STRENGTH:

Lives Touched By Cystinosis

STRENGTH:
Lives Touched By Cystinosis

Copyright © 2017 by Cystinosis Research Network
www.cystinosis.org
Cover design by Amanda Leigh
Formatting by Leigh Designs

Strength / Cystinosis Research Network – 1st ed. =
Library of Congress Cataloging-in-Publication Data
ISBN-13: 978-1548540876 | ISBN-10: 1548540870

DEDICATION

This book is dedicated to the entire cystinosis community … the patients, their parents, caregivers, family, friends, doctors.

INTRODUCTION

A disease is considered rare if it affects fewer than 1 in 2,000 people. Out of roughly 7.4 billion people in this world, those diagnosed with cystinosis amounts to only about 2,000. That is extremely rare. So rare, that there are a large number of doctors and nurses who have never heard of it. Or, perhaps it was briefly discussed during medical school but they were told they shouldn't worry too much about it because they probably wouldn't see it. And in all honesty, yes, those chances are quite slim.

But there are more than just 2,000 worldwide who are affected by cystinosis. Parents, grandparents, aunts, uncles, siblings, friends and caregivers of those with this disease are also affected. Together we are one community. Banded together through our shared experiences, quests to raise awareness, and commitment to funding research. No two persons with cystinosis are alike. We each walk our own unique path but there are similarities to be found.

What began as an idea to help spread awareness quickly morphed into the collection you are about to read. The stories that have come from our community paint a picture of what life is like for so many of us. While they share certain aspects the stories are all different, making up a mosaic of our life experiences. There are many challenges we have faced and many times we have all felt alone. Like no one else could ever truly know what we were going though. It is our hope that this collection will bring support and understanding to the cystinosis community and beyond. A talisman to read and hold on to when we're feeling overwhelmed.

Through struggle there is also much hope to be found. As we read these stories the themes of perseverance and optimism became quickly apparent. They say adversity creates opportunity. The opportunity to become stronger; to choose how you want to view the world. Time and again the cystinosis community has chosen to rise and attempt to overcome the obstacles that lay in our path. The road is long and full of hurdles, but we are still here and we are still fighting.

This collection seeks to shine a light on some of the everyday people in this fight. Whether fighting for their friends and loved ones or fighting the disease itself, they do not fight alone. The stories contained within this book will showcase many sides of our experiences. All of the brave contributors have shared a piece of themselves. Their vulnerability and strength attests to the endurance of their spirits and the cystinosis community as a whole. We would like to thank all of the contributors for helping us create such a powerful letter to the world.

We hope you enjoy all of the pieces that are to come and share in our highs and our lows. Information on how you can help support the cystinosis community and join our supporters can be found at the end of this collection. Thank you for being here and for helping us spread our strength to all of the communities across the globe.

FOREWORD

Dr. Paul Goodyer
Professor of Pediatrics and Human Genetics
McGill University Health Centre

Across the world, about 1 in every 200 people silently carry some type of mutation in the CTNS gene on chromosome 17. When, by chance two CTNS "carriers" marry and have children, 25% of the offspring inherit the two dysfunctional CTNS gene and develop cystinosis. This makes cystinosis an ultra-rare disease, occurring in every 100-200 thousand people. The cardinal features of cystinosis were gradually worked out by physicians in the early 20th century. Aberhalden first described a Swiss child who died at 21 months of age with widespread cystine crystals in the major organs. However, it was not until 1924, that the Dutch Pathologist, George Lignac, provided a clear description of the cardinal features of the disease (rickets, renal disease and severe growth failure in early life). In 1931, a Swiss pediatrician, Guido Fanconi, recognized that the earliest manifestations of cystinosis are caused by the massive urinary loss of phosphate, bicarbonate and other crucial electrolytes which are normally reabsorbed by the renal tubules. By replacing these urinary losses oral, physicians learned to offset symptoms caused by the renal Fanconi syndrome, but this did not avert progressive renal failure by the end of the first decade of life. Another major step forward came in the 1970's, when it was shown that successful renal transplantation was possible in cystinosis – propelling many patients into young adulthood.

The modern understanding of cystinosis is founded on two key discoveries. Firstly, in the 1980`s, American investigators at the NIH showed that abnormal cystine accumulation occurs because of a defect in the channel through which cystine exits the cell`s lysosomes; these small subcellular compartments serve as re-cycling centers that constantly degrade old proteins into their constituent amino acids (including cystine) for reuse. Since cystine is unable to exit the lysosome, levels progressively increase until the point where cystine comes out of solution, forming crystals and disrupting the biology of the cell. This observation led to the discovery that chemicals such as cysteamine could convert cystine into a smaller compound that can leave the lysosome through alternative normal channels. Nesterova and Gahl recently estimated that every year of strict cysteamine treatment yields a one-year delay in the need for renal transplantation.

The second important discovery came in 1998, when a consortium of investigators including Town and Antignac identified the cystinosis gene (CTNS) on chromosome 17. This confirmed that the CTNS gene encodes a protein (cystinosin) that forms the lysosomal cystine channel and that there are over 100 different CTNS gene mutations which have arisen throughout the world over many years. The most common of these mutations involves a large deletion of DNA (including the CTNS gene) that apparently arose in an individual of Germanic ancestry in about 500 AD. This same mutation is present in about 40-50% of cystinosis cases in Northern Europe and has been spread via migration to North America (seen primarily in children of German or British ancestry), southern Europe South America and the Middle East. Many other CTNS gene mutations have arisen over many years in many parts of the world where they may be confined within a single family or spread across larger regions of the world. For example, a new CTNS mutation was transferred by an Irish immigrant to the French Canadian community in the early 18th or 19th century; this mutation now accounts for 40-50% of cystinosis in Quebec. Interestingly, some patients with clinically milder forms of cystinosis have been found to harbour less disruptive mutations of the CTNS gene, explaining why some individuals have relatively late onset of the Fanconi Syndrome or why some have only corneal crystals without kidney involvement.

With each of these advances, remarkable contributions have been made by the cystinosis community, itself. At an early stage, passionate leaders from cystinosis families organized support groups and research foundations to engage the medical research community in North America and Europe. Early volunteers underwent skin biopsies to generate the fibroblasts cell lines used for observations regarding cystine depletion by cysteamine. DNA samples provided by European patients led to the discovery of the CTNS gene. Critically, many North American patients volunteered for the first trials of oral cysteamine which showed oral cysteamine could improve growth and delay kidney transplantation; follow-up studies established the benefits for hypothyroidism and later complications. Patient volunteers also made possible the first trials of topical cysteamine for corneal crystals and the development of a delayed release form of cysteamine. By supporting international patient registries, cystinosis patients have positioned themselves to educate new generations of patients and physicians and encourage clinical trials of novel therapies.

While we tend to focus on "breakthroughs", it is important to recognize the slow and incremental progress that has been made in practical, day-to-day aspects of patient care. To a great extent, this has been accomplished largely by the cystinosis patient groups. Regular local, national and international meetings have offered the chance for patients to share knowledge about managing the many drugs needed to treat renal Fanconi, how to access specialized public services and how to help each family cope with the disease. Transition from pediatric to adult medical services has been identified as a crucial issue that must be addressed.

Despite this past progress, all would agree that there are major unmet needs in cystinosis. Strict adherence to six-hourly dosing is difficult. Data from the CureCystinosis registry indicate that at least 20% of patients report they have taken "a holiday" from treatment at some point – 5% have stopped cysteamine for over 1 year. Thus, the advent of a delayed release (X2/day) form of cysteamine holds great promise. In North America, 40-50% of patients have taken the delayed release form of cysteamine, reporting improvement in quality of life scores. Stablized cysteamine eyedrops are now available and a number of delayed release ophthalmic preparations are in development.

There is also increasing evidence that some aspects of cystinosis cannot be cured by chemical mobilization of intra-lysosomal cystine. Cysteamine does not reverse Fanconi Syndrome and can delay but doesn't eliminate the eventual need for renal transplantation. Cherqui has proposed that it may be possible to harvest blood stem cells from the patient's bone marrow, add the normal gene to these cells in the laboratory and then re-infuse them into the patient. This strategy requires the use of chemotherapeutic agents to eliminate the remaining mutant cells in bone marrow but studies in Ctns mutant mice have shown great promise. Other investigators are working on ways to introduce the normal CTNS gene directly into patient tissues with viral delivery systems. Finally, some groups have recently postulated that loss of the cystinosin protein may disturb important cell functions beyond its role as a cystine channel in lysosomes. Thus Emma and others have begun to screen known drugs for the ability to restore some of these other cell functions – perhaps to be used in combination cysteamine.

Whatever the future holds for cystinosis, it will be the result of a concerted partnership between investigators, patient foundations, pharmaceutical companies, research funding organizations and the courage of individual patients and their families. This collection of stories illustrates why we are all involved.

Ethan's Story

This was written by Jennifer Bartkowski and Ethan Bartkowski on behalf of Ethan Bartkowski:

My name is Ethan and I am a 7 year old boy from New Berlin, Wisconsin. I live with my dad, Ross, my mom, Jennifer, my little brother, Jackson, and my dog, Morgan. Most of my life is living like other 7 year old kids, but what you don't see with the naked eye is that my body is battling a disease called cystinosis. The disease only affects 500 people in the United States and 2000 people in the entire world. The disease is where cystine crystals accumulate on my organs and my body is not able to fight off these little crystals so they will eventually cause the organs to shut down. Most people have no idea what cystinosis is or anything about it, so it is constantly a learning opportunity for everyone I come in contact with. This can be frustrating but ultimately I know that I am helping pave the way for younger kids that have cystinosis so they will receive better care and under-standing when they explain to doctors, nurses, teachers, family, friends, etc that they have a very rare disease called cystinosis.

I am lucky enough that I have a close friend named Mason Stilke, who is 13 and from Elkhorn, Wisconsin and also has cystinosis. We get together with our parents at least once a month and we enjoy a lot of the same things. Skylanders, Legos, Minecraft, video games, etc., so I look forward to every time we get to hang out. Even though I have other friends at school and in my family, Mason experiences a lot of the same things that I have to deal with daily which makes us have a special bond. My little brother Jackson, who is 3, does not have cystinosis but is very supportive of me. He constantly follows me around and wants to be a part of everything that I do. He even mimics me when I am getting my medicine through my g-tube and has my mom and dad pretend to give him medicine through his belly button. As I get older I am becoming more and more informed about my disease and realizing that this is my "normal," even though some people will never understand how this can be "normal." I was diagnosed at 21 months and I don't remember experiencing life without medications every 3-6 hours (even through the night), a constant unquenchable thirst, eye drops given every waking hour to avoid crystal accumulation on my eyes, not being able to sweat, muscle wasting, fragile bones, etc. Although most people would not call me lucky, I know that I am fortunate to have wonderful people in my life that stand by me and help my family out when they need it. From our wonderful family to our amazing friends we are truly blessed.

Although I may have times that I complain and do not want to take my medicine or eye drops, I know that this is what I need to live. My family backs me in everything I want to do and as I get older I know that they will always be my biggest supporters. Whether it is getting over my fear of heights, not being able to play football because of the physical aspect needed in the game, my many doctor appointments, my unorthodox way of eating, not being able to spend the night at friends' houses because an adult needs to give me my medications in my tube during the night, wearing sunglasses all of the time because of my sensitivity to light, I could go on and on... but I know that these things make me who I am today and who I will be tomorrow. They may be stressful and discouraging at times, but as I overcome each obstacle I am making myself a better person.

I have high hopes that one day there will be more manageable medications or even a cure for cystinosis. My family continues to stay informed and they do every-thing they can to keep my disease at bay, which will hopefully mean a longer and healthier life than those people in previous decades that have had to battle cystinosis. They all were such strong individuals and I hope that I will continue to show my strength as I get older and be an advocate for all of those people in the cystinosis community.

Some of the life lessons that my family has learned through the ups and downs are that you can never expect the unexpected. When you envision your life one way, something is bound to throw in a curve ball and derail you from your plans. Think of the end goal and do whatever you have to, making sure you achieve whatever it is that you desire. Don't sweat the small stuff in life because there is enough big stuff to worry about. Lastly, there will always be someone that has it worse so stay positive and remember it will get better.

Some quotes that my family tries to live by each and every day are:

"Life consists not in holding good cards but in playing those you hold well."
Josh Billings

"May you live all the days of your life."
Jonathan Swift

A Letter to Cystinosis
by Samantha Beckwith

Dear Cystinosis,

My parents first found out about you when I was three. They cried, but I obviously didn't understand at that age. They were told that they might outlive me. They finally found out why I didn't eat properly, and why I drank so much.

My sister was born about a year later, and you were mentioned again. My mum told me a story once, of how on our way to hospital I'd know whether or not I was going to clinic or for a blood test, because of the turning we took. My second home is still the hospital sometimes – but, I'm 19 now and go to my appointments independently. I miss the children's clinic, even though there's never really anyone the same as me there. I was always the oldest one there, but now I'm the youngest in the waiting room.

I had my kidney transplant in 2010, and always got told how amazing you feel after it, but more tablets and due to still having cystinosis I didn't really get that.

But, you know what, cystinosis? I lead a great life! In 2012, you meant that I could meet my favourite band –

One Direction. I've met some amazing people through online life, and I've found love and happiness in certain things that get me through hospital.

I work almost full time now, at a nursery. If anyone ever tells you that you can't do something, smile and say, "Sure I can!"

I've made some amazing memories in my life so far, and I plan to make many more. We've come so far in the medical world that my parents no longer have to worry about what the doctors told them sixteen years ago. I've met some lovely nurses and doctors, who've helped me feel better and made me smile. I have met fellow cystinosis patients – whether online, or in person – who are equally as great. They're strong, I'm strong. Together we'll fight, and one day see a cure for our future children.

Dear Cystinosis, you may have made me who I am today... But, I won't let you hold me back.

Follow Samantha's blog at
www.cystinosissam.blogspot.ca

I Hope He Knows
by Amanda Buck

The alarm goes off at 7:20am. I have 10 minutes before my 3-year-old needs her medicine. I hate waking her up for meds, I wish she could sleep as long as she needs. Before I can dwell on this I hear my 10-month old son start to cry, time to get up.

He greets me with the most beautiful smile and a laugh that seems to say, "Oh hey, there you are. Did you know I was calling for you?" My heart melts. Time is running out and I can't feed him immediately so I pick him up, grab the meds and head to my daughter's room. He starts crying and squirming in my arms, trying to find his favourite food source. Poor guy, I wish I could instantly ease his hunger instead of prolonging it. I hope he knows how much I love him.

I sit beside her on the bed and cradle him in my arms. Finally, he's able to nurse. Gently I try to wake my daughter, but she is not in the mood. Thrashing and whining that she doesn't want to take her medicine. I don't blame her, it tastes foul and makes her nauseous. But, I remind her, it keeps her healthy so she can continue to run around and play with her friends. She doesn't care, she's three after all, long term advantages don't mean much.

She's getting worked up, kicking and hitting the wall, her bed, me and her brother. I have to stop him mid feed, put him on the floor for safety and then try to calm his sister. My son's cry fills the room, protesting that he wants more. My heart aches for his struggle but his sister needs some support right now. She needs to calm down and take her time sensitive medication.

After she's relaxed a bit and taken her meds I immediately pick my son up and continue to nurse. He makes adorable little sounds, sighs of contentment that he's finally back where he wants to be, snuggled with mom and eating, his happy place. I stroke his face and hair softly then put my forefinger in the palm of his hand so he can grab on. I gently rub my thumb over the back of his hand.

Suddenly my daughter gives a cough. Not a clearing her throat or fighting a cold cough but an, "I might get sick," cough. After two years of living with cystinosis and taking awful medicine, I know that cough well. I desperately hope that she can hold off at least until her body has had enough time to absorb the meds.

We go downstairs and I ask my daughter to lie on the couch and watch tv. If she stays still and doesn't get worked up there's a chance she won't get sick. If she'll eat some food that's even better. I let my son down and off he goes, patrolling the area for anything he can get his hands on, the more off limits the better. Then he's pulling himself up on the couch trying to grab and play with his sister. My happy, busy little boy.

In the kitchen while making breakfast I watch them through the pass-through. My daughter's feet dangling off the couch. My son standing at the patio door, leaning against the glass and smacking his chubby little hands against it. Occasionally he presses his face to the glass, just for a taste, laughing to himself afterwards. It must be nice to be amused by everything.

Despite the rocky start to the morning his laughter and good mood are infectious. He gives me a sense of calm and happiness, despite my worries for the nauseous little girl on the couch. I hope he knows how much that means to me.

I let my daughter eat her eggs, 1 of only 10 or so foods she will consent to eat, on the couch. Anything I can do to keep her from getting sick. My son goes in the high chair for some baby mush the package says is oatmeal. He lunges for the spoon immediately and continuously between every bite, like he just can't get enough. The difference in appetite between my children is almost comical. As I look over to see my daughter pick the tiniest piece of egg she can find and very slowly chew, it's comforting to know that at least my son has a rich and varied diet. Maybe I'm not a total failure.

Seconds after taking my son out of the high chair, my daughter suddenly sprints into the kitchen, hands tightly clasped over her mouth. My heart sinks as I realize that all our efforts have been in vain. Leaving him hastily on the ground I go after her and find a bowl to place on the floor. I hold her hair away from her tiny face and gently rub her back while she loses the little amount of food she'd eaten. At least it's been well over 30 minutes since she had her meds. I won't have to administer them again.

Tired of being left to his own devices, my son chooses this very moment to need me too. He's crying and leaning into me, grabbing and clutching to try make it clear that he wants up now. If only I could comfort both of my children together, but she's still sick and getting upset that her brother is literally stepping over her to get to me. I hope he knows how much I want to comfort him as well.

Afterwards she starts to feels much better so I'm able to pick up my son and we all sit together and watch some more tv. He's able to be close to me while he plays and she's able to lie close to me while she gets some rest. Later, when it's just me and my son in his room, I rock him in my arms and sing to him before nap time. Today I hold him a little bit closer, smell his hair and try to commit this moment to memory. My beautiful, squishy baby boy, leaning his head into my chest, so full of curiosity and laughter. Easy going and loving.

I worry that he feels left out when my daughter needs some extra attention. Maybe he doesn't realize just how special he is. Special to me, to his dad and especially to his sister. I'll never be able to fully articulate the kind of joy and wonder that he's brought to this family. I hope he knows how important that is, how important he is, and how much his family loves him, now and forever.

Follow Amanda's blog at www.elsinosis.com

ELSIE - Living Life on a Carousel
By Charlie Buck

I fell in love with Elsie the day she was born; such a beautiful little girl with a shock of dark hair. This is my beloved Granddaughter and I am her primary caregiver when her parents are at work. When she was 6 months old, she stopped growing. Deep down, I thought that something was wrong, but just did not know what it could be. Despite everything, she seemed to be developing okay, just not getting any taller, so I thought it must be in her genetic makeup as her maternal Grandparents are not tall. She was this miniature person that brought such joy into our lives.

One day, our Son and Daughter-in-Law insisted on coming over to see us and would not take no for an answer. It was an unusual request because we don't have set times to visit each other - we just drop in when-ever. It was such a shock when they told us that Elsie had been diagnosed with cystin-something-or-other. I could not take it all in. My husband, I know, wasn't taking it all in either. All we knew was that this beautiful little girl, our Granddaughter, had something missing in her genetic makeup that currently cannot be cured, and if left untreated, would be fatal. Even worse, this genetic missing link is so rare. The hardest part of all is that we are to blame. One of us is the carrier of this missing link.

We have, unwittingly, passed this on to Elsie through our Son. I was right about it being a genetic issue, but wrong in thinking it was something as simple as height (and oh, how I wish that it was something as simple as height).

Since then, we have lived in the shadow of cystinosis. A constant reminder is all the medication she has to take to prevent that dreadful word - fatal. We have also become educated on what cystinosis is all about and what we can expect as Elsie grows up. It's hard to read about. The most enlightening part is that, with compliance, she will grow up. Research is going in leaps and bounds and I believe that in her lifetime, there could even be a cure.

Her life is like a carousel. Some days are amazing and the carousel is so much fun. She eats nearly all that is given her, she downs her medicines with seeming relish and her laughter can be heard throughout the house. On other days the carousel is making her feel sick, her "barf bowl" is close at hand, she has no appetite and her medicines taste, "yucky." On those days we take a back-seat to cystinosis, we cuddle and do quiet things and when those days are over, I go home, make a cup of tea and silently weep.

It's not all doom and gloom. She is an amazing individual and even at three years old, she is very independent and strong willed. She is a leader. She is also like every precious three year old. She is loving and caring, she loves to help, she can be a fantastic big Sister (then other times not!), she can act out, she can have tantrums and yes, she can wind both her Grandpas and her Daddy around her little finger, just like every three year old little girl, and we all love her all the more for it!

I don't know what Elsie's future will be like. I can only hope that she will have a long, happy and healthy one.

Hope is a very special word to me and one that I hold close to my heart. After all, Elsie's middle name is, you guessed it, **Hope**.

Silly Grandpa
by Chris Buck

How could we know the journey we were about to embark on that sunny August day when we all met at the hospital in anticipation of the arrival of our first grandchild. Were we being given a hint when the proud parents announced the name, Elsie Hope? We never dreamt where this would take us. As with most children with cystinosis there was no hint, we gathered in the room taking turns to hold our new little bundle of joy, taking pictures, laughing and joking in the intoxicating atmosphere of unbridled joy.

As time went on we all fussed and worried over every milestone, met, unmet or nearly so it made little difference. Alert and attentive there was never a hint our little girl could have anything but a bright normal future ahead as the collective grandparents fussed and spoilt her at every opportunity. Then came that day when they brought her to our home and quietly, almost apologetically, gave us the news that our little angel had this thing called cystinosis. They gave us the brief summary of what it was and what it might mean, "What did you call it? Cystin-what?" We had never heard of it, didn't know anything about it and at that time didn't want to. "What do you mean she is not perfect, sorry you made a mistake, of course she is perfect, they have it wrong, can't be, never, not our Elsie." I have crashed a car and motor-bike, run into poles, fallen into holes, got knocked off my bike, watched both my parents die of cancer as well as a host of other mishaps, but never has anything or anyone ever got close to hitting me as hard as I took one that day. My complete sense of balance was upended, I had no place to put down a reference, awash in my sorrow and bewilderment I crawled off to bed that night and let the tears of sorrow, frustration, and hopelessness flow like water down my face in an unending cascade I thought could never end. I would later find out, not only would it end but our little lady would show us what I should have known but needed this special gift to find out.

As she started to talk and interact with us I took great delight in being foolish with her. As she learned her colours I would change them around, "No grandpa, it's blue" she would tell me as I asked if it was pink! My wife would scold me and say to her, "Is Grandpa being silly?" To which she would look at me with her radiant smile and say, "Silly Grandpa." As time went by she learned about trips to the hospital to take blood and those eye drops that stung so fiercely, the medication that made her throw up to name just a few of the trials she endured. I watched and worried as to how she would cope and yes, I fretted she was getting all the care she needed to grow and develop.

I have been an engineer for a long time, engineers fix problems, we even like to fix problems, it's what we are good at, but try like I have never done in my life, I can't fix this one. I would happily give up all the other fixes in my life if I could fix this one, but I can't. Since I can't fix it I have to learn to live with it, it's like growing old. I was at the back of the line when patience was being allocated so my stores were used up a long time ago. I don't remember when it was that I got used to it, but I have, and since then I have got used to a lot of things I didn't want to, losing my hair, flexibility, strength, eyesight are just a few examples. So what about getting used to cystinosis? I really don't want to get used to it, I want it gone, now, forever. Problem is, for now at least, it hasn't gone so I have got to get used to it and make the most of every day, just like getting old. Unlike getting old there is hope that one day it will be gone, so now I hope I don't get so old that I don't see the day cystinosis is gone for good for everyone. Hope is part of her name, she will prevail.

For now I am rewarded with a wonderful little girl who brings untold joy and pleasure to everyone. Her vitality, spirit and strength of character is so strong that cystinosis or not, I am shown every day that the real value of life is to take each day and cherish it as if it were our last, one day it surely will be.

I could easily have learned this lesson without cystinosis but I am not sure I would have.

Silly Grandpa.

"Our New Normal"

Our story of our daughter, Charlotte Ellie Coe
Written by Michael & Megan Coe
Diagnosed at 13 months old in November of 2015

She is our first and only child, dreamed about and talked
about for years before she was born. It seems like
yesterday and a past life in the same moment; day-
dreaming of our daughter's future, a scene before my
mind's eye of a bright eyed toddler running around with
friends, growing stronger every day. I could almost hear
her laughing that true laughter that only children un-
touched by the world's woes can embrace. As I sat in the
waiting room, pushing my fears to the back of my mind
and staring at my beautiful girl, I imagined these things
once more. I tried to imagine reclaiming those hopes, I
imagined her long hair trailing behind her as she ran
through the grass, careless and far from the hospital
waiting room. I held tight to the images, trying to will them
into the world against the realities we had been living for
the past several months.

"We are ready to take her in now. Will Dad be coming in too?" the surgeon said. "Yes" I said with a watery-eyed smile and a knot in my throat. I wanted Charlotte to see my smile and hear my voice as she fell asleep. I didn't want her to be afraid or alone, I wanted to sing her to sleep like she's used to at home. '...Just this one last thing and Charlotte will grow...' I thought. Just this one last nightmare and things will return to normal; she will run and sing and play, I told myself. As we entered the bright room, I began to sing. I sang past the lump in my throat as the surgeons hooked up the anesthesia. I stared into her bright blue eyes, and watched as their spark faded and her head rolled to the side in deep sleep.

Our normal disappeared last summer when things abruptly started to change. Just as my wife and I began to feel as though life couldn't be more perfect, just as we began to feel comfortable and confident in our roles as new parents, it became clear something wasn't quite right. At first we were merely confused; Charlotte had been growing right along the upper end of the growth chart at all her checkups. Then we noticed a slowing in her growth, something difficult to understand. Charlotte had no problem nursing and had been trying different foods for the past several months. As we continued different strategies, and interventions to try and get Charlotte to gain weight, more time passed. Although Charlotte's cognitive development continued, her weight, strength and physical milestones were at a standstill. The term "failure to thrive" was added to our vocabulary; an ugly term if you ask me. As a parent, the term made me feel ashamed and incompetent. Had we failed to make our child thrive? We pushed harder, made the switch from breastfeeding to a high calorie formula blend. No weight gain, still pale, each passing day of worry and frustration taking pieces of our happiness away.

Odd instances of vomiting were occurring. "Babies throw up," the nurses told us. But it was strange, even as a newborn Charlotte rarely threw up. The vomiting had us presenting to the emergency room on multiple occasions. "She's just sick. As long as she isn't dehydrated take her home to rest." We heard this time and time again. The frustration we felt was both quelled and fueled by nurses trying to comfort our concerns, "you're new parents, it's normal for kids to get sick," they'd say, but our instincts were in conflict. An overwhelming feeling that there was something more going on had us reeling with worry and fear. This instinct eventually led us to demand tests; they had to do something, anything other than turn her away again. There was a nagging feeling that something beyond just the flu or a cold was at play, and we needed answers.

So they took a blood and urine sample and within hours we were told to return immediately to the ER. They needed to test for diabetes as her urine had large amounts of abnormal nutrients present upon testing. We administered antibiotics to remedy a bladder infection, which only partially explained the composition of nutrients in her urine. The vomiting continued to persist and Charlotte stopped eating solids altogether, a follow up appointment showed continued nutrient loss in her urine. We watched as doctors scratched their heads, and after several follow up appointments without a diagnosis, we were finally admitted to the pediatric unit for an extended stay so that a team of doctors could perform multiple tests and observations to try and figure out what exactly was going on. Again the doctors scratched their heads, until the 3rd morning of our stay, after multiple blood and urine draws, observations at every meal, and a dozen consultations; we were discharged to the care of a pediatric nephrologist. We were given supplements to try and balance Charlotte's electrolyte levels, and feared that the infection might have damaged her kidneys; we were hopeful that maybe they would just heal over time and things would return to normal. We never once thought that there wasn't a fix, a cure, to what was happening with our little girl. Yet, at our next appointment the nephrologist took a blood sample and explained that she would send it to San Diego to test for a rare genetic disease called cystinosis. Over the coming months, our lives would be turned upside down, forever changed.

Deep breaths, waiting, I stared at my wife, pale as a bedsheet in the grips of fear as we sat in the surgery waiting room. Almost 4 months had passed since the call came from the nurse, "your daughter has cystinosis, your doctor is out of town but we need to schedule an appoint-ment as soon as possible." Just thinking back to that moment I began to shake with the old feelings of that time. I pushed the thought aside, we had grown so much stronger in the past few months and the past was just an echo of the present. I brought myself back to the present and took a deep breath. Slowly I thought of all the times we had to struggle to get Charlotte to take her supple-ments, the gagging, the vomit, the tears we shed after she went down for a nap or to bed in the evening. I took another deep breath and brought myself back to the room once more. After 2 hours of struggling between grieving thoughts of the past few months and the hopeful thoughts of tomorrow, the surgeon entered the room. "She did great, the g-tube is in place and she is in recovery," the surgeon said. Relief washed over my wife, Megan, and I as we hugged and followed a nurse down to the recovery room.

My eyelids grow heavy as I pull the plunger back on the last syringe of this week's medication. Prepping them every Sunday has made our day to day feel less medical, even though we push 105 syringes of medication into her stomach each week, the button on her stomach that allows us to do so feels like a part of her. Thinking back to the waiting room as she had the g-tube placed I couldn't have thought that we would come to appreciate the little wonder so much. I wouldn't have pictured myself setting up a "chemistry lab" in the living room each Sunday to prepare and label over 105 syringes of 6 different prescriptions. I wouldn't have imagined that a task like that could be rewarding, almost soothing in a way. The repetitive motion of pulling back syringes like meditation, peaceful in the simplicity of the action in spite of the overarching complexity of cystinosis itself. I meditate on the friends our family has made along this journey thus far. Fast lifelong friends that understand the road behind us, and the path ahead that is full of uncertainty. My gratitude for friends that Charlotte can grow alongside and not feel so alone in the rarity of cystinosis. I meditate on the goals ahead, and appreciate that the darkness is lifted far enough to think ahead again and not just think about the emergency of the moment. When things seem dark it is easy to think negatively, it is the path of least resistance. Amongst our many trials we have strived to hold on to the positive and to approach each challenge with love and courage as Charlotte does. As I finish my normal Sunday routine of prepping medications for the week ahead I pause to appreciate that this is our normal routine. Not normal necessarily, but our "new normal" as we sometimes say. In our new normal we have learned to find the silver lining in every challenge and we have learned to truly embrace life's joyous moments and not take them for granted. Beside me I hear a noise coming through the baby monitor; Charlotte is standing in her crib bouncing as she sings "juice, juice, juice!" I watch as she bends down and places her hands in front of her feet and yells "yoga!" As I enter her room I pause to appreciate that she is finally growing stronger, and then I hand her a cup of juice, as I normally do.

Kian's Story
By Roseann Cotter

Kian was diagnosed with cystinosis in November 2015, when he was just thirteen months old. He became ill just after his first birthday with severe vomiting, dehydration, leaking kidneys, loss of appetite and weight loss. Kian was admitted to Mercy University Hospital in Cork where he spent nearly three weeks. The doctors there suspected cystinosis almost right away, as they had other patients with cystinosis and recognised the symptoms, but also suspected he may have some type of kidney disease. We couldn't believe what we were being told, when he was admitted we had just thought it was something viral and he would be back to himself in no time. Never did we imagine that our little boy could possibly have an incurable disease.

His doctors did a blood test for cystinosis, which was sent to the UK for testing. Kian was then transferred to Temple Street Children's Hospital in Dublin as they are more specialised there with cystinosis. Again they did some blood tests along with a bone x-ray to check for rickets (which thankfully he didn't have), and saw an Ophthalmologist to check for crystals in his eyes (which he also didn't have), both possible indicators of cystinosis. We had spent ten days there when the doctors confirmed that Kian in fact had cystinosis, which was confirmed by raised cystine levels in his blood. Although we were aware that Kian could have it and were informed of what it meant for him, our whole world fell apart. Nothing could have prepared us for the devastation of having it confirmed. Before then we had never even heard of cystinosis and so many thoughts were going through our minds. The fear of what our beautiful baby boy would have to go through, what effects it would have on his life and would he be in pain?

We look at our son's precious happy smiling face and how strong and brave he has been and that's what gets us through every day. If he could do it, as small as he is, then so could we. Kian gets supplementary feeds along with all his medication through an NG tube. He is currently waiting to get a PEG in his stomach. He stills eats very little and only drinks water. Trying to get the weight on him has been our biggest struggle so far. He has good days mostly apart from the few hospital admissions and weekly blood draws, but even with all of this it never gets the better of him he just keeps smiling through it all.

Kian also has four older brothers Troy, Evan, Dean and Rhys. He adores them as they do him. Kian loves music and dancing, no matter what music it is, he has them all up dancing. They're all great with him and always make sure to give him a kiss and cuddle every day and tell him how much he's loved.

Kian is now sixteen months old. He's cruising but not walking yet. His speech is not great, he has only three words, and while I'm not overly concerned just yet as he is still very young, I have referred him to early intervention just to get him that extra little help that he might need. Although Kian is not on the full dose of medication yet, we are slowly working him up to it. Cystagon can be hard on the stomach but it doesn't seem to affect him very much. We try to take each day as it comes and not think too much of the future at the moment.

We are very hopeful for a cure so Kian and everyone else living with this condition can have the cystinosis free life they deserve. Words can't describe enough how proud we are of our little warrior everyday. He never fails to put a smile on our face and we are truly blessed to have such a beautiful little boy in our lives.

Kelsey's Story
Kelsey Cunningham

Imagine your life as the back of an immaculately packed moving truck. Everything you are, and every piece of your life is stored in boxes, perfectly stacked from the floor to the ceiling. There is just enough room to fit everything in, and everything has its place. The diagnosis of cystinosis is like looking up at the back of that beautifully packed truck, only to realize you forgot to pack the deep-freeze. So, you shuffle those picture perfect boxes and try to make room for this incredibly inconvenient new piece of your life. To do that, some of those boxes, those pieces of you, have to be left behind.

I will not say that I am who I am today because of cystinosis, but I will say that cystinosis has played (and continues to play) a large role in my life. Making room for the deep-freeze was like anything significant in life, a process. I was fourteen years old when my brother, Andrew, was diagnosed with cystinosis. I can remember the exact moment that I was told what the diagnosis was. My dad and I were sitting in the cafeteria of the old Alberta Children's Hospital. I remember asking if they knew why Andrew was so sick, and my dad telling me it was not the diagnosis they were hoping for. I remember looking down at my half eaten grilled cheese sandwich and saying, "If we have a name, then we know what it is. If we know what it is, we can treat it. We can handle it. That's good."

There are two types of people in this world. Those who look at the freezer and see a heavy burden; cumbersome and taking up too much space, and, those who look at the freezer and see nothing but potential for all the delicious popsicles it can hold. I've seen many families get sucked into the black-hole of negativity that is the diagnosis of a chronic disease. They throw everything off of the truck and take only the freezer. They throw away every piece of who they are because of the disease, until their entire identity is the diagnosis. Finding space for our freezer was not an easy task, but my parents did a phenomenal job of making sure we had everything we needed in the truck after it was repacked. If we were going to make space for a deep-freeze, we might as well fill it with popsicles first.

At the end of 2015 I was deep in the crux of a quarter-life crisis and had no idea what to do with myself. I quit my job of four years to fast track my bachelors degree in Social Work, finished my practicum, and found myself for the first time in my adult life having no idea what was coming next. With nothing to lose, I decided to take some chances and see where I landed. I applied for jobs all over Canada, and decided late one night to see what opportunities Ireland might have for me as well. I was aimlessly scrolling through volunteer positions on LinkedIn when the position of an 'Executive Committee Member' caught my eye. I opened the posting up, and halfway through the introductory paragraph read that Cystinosis Ireland was looking for a member with experience in family support, fundraising, and building international relations. I was ecstatic! I sent off my application and within a matter of hours had a response! Two days later, I bought my tickets, and two months later I moved to Dublin.

Now, many people might think that I am crazy upping my entire life and moving halfway across the world for a volunteer position, but, my favourite way to travel is by the seat of my pants. When you're given that bright of a sign from the universe, you've got to take a chance! What started as a volunteer position has turned into a full time career. My position is generously gifted to the charity by an outside benefactor, meaning that I get to do work for the charity without my wages being taken out of the donations. Every euro goes towards improving the lives of those living with cystinosis in Ireland.

A few years ago my mom asked me what my dream job would be, and without any hesitation my answer was "I'd love to be Zoe Solsby!" (Vice President of the Cystinosis Research Foundation). My dream job is to be working with the families of those living with Cystinosis, helping to raise money and awareness, while supporting groundbreaking research, all in the effort of finding a cure. I want my brother, Andrew, and every person with cystinosis to have the best life possible. I view my position with Cystinosis Ireland as my chance to do everything I can to help eradicate this disease. I'd love to find myself unemployed again, all because we found the cure for cystinosis. My new job is the jumbo-popsicle in the deep-freeze, and I am incredibly grateful to be able to enjoy it while I can!

My mom always says to, "find the silver-linings," and I try to do just that. Cystinosis may have changed our lives, but not all the changes have been bad. I get to live in a country I've always wanted to call home, working in my absolute dream job, for a cause I am incredibly passionate about, and it is all thanks to cystinosis. My life did not become the disease, but the disease did help me to shape my life. I don't know what pieces of myself I had to give up in order to make room for the deep-freeze, but I figure if I can't name them, I didn't need them in the first place.

Highs and Lows of Cystinosis
By Kayla Drury

I was diagnosed with Cystinosis at 18 months old. I am now 28. I have not had a transplant yet, despite doctors saying I would need one by the time I was 10. I believe a big part of this is due to Cystagon. This is a medication used to slow the effects of cystinosis. I started Cystagon before I can remember and it used to make me very sick and it also has a pungent smell like rotting cabbage. This was not just me these were common side effects of the drug.

I remember being sent home from school many times after being quite violently sick. I would fight it the best I could, my mum would tell me to count to 10 and try to distract me, and sometimes this worked, at least for a while, maybe long enough for me to have absorbed some of it. However, sometimes it still came back up later when I got to school. Over the years with much determination and often arguments with my parents, I built up a stronger tolerance to Cystagon. At secondary school I was still sick maybe every few weeks and after secondary school it got even better. I got stronger at fighting it and I built up a tolerance over many years.

I believe the biggest reason for me getting to where I am today and not needing a transplant until now is purely down to Cystagon and my parent's determination.

As I said I am now 28. I have just been referred to the transplant team and am starting to look for a kidney match. Things are not going quite so good. I am struggleing to continue my fight with Cystagon, as my stomach is not as strong as it used to be, and I now have severe IBS and reflux/acid heartburn. The doctors are trying to get me the new delayed release Cystagon, Procysbi, but this could take some time. My kidneys are functioning at about 20% though they said because I am very small that it could be less, as they may be overestimating it. My renal tubes are leaking more and I'm struggling to keep up. I drink over a litre of water every night and wake up 3 times to go to the toilet. I also have to take huge amounts of potassium and other electrolyte supplements as I lose so much where my renal tubes are leaking.

The very biggest affect for me, however, is the way I feel. A few years ago I used to just get tired easily, now I just am excessively tired and fatigued every day. Tiredness is horrible, it makes you less tolerant and it makes you miss out on things with your friends because you're too tired. It has even made me fall out with a friend and stopped me from being her bridesmaid because I was too tired to keep up. Tiredness even affects your mind. It makes it hard to think or make decisions and sometimes you feel sad when you should be feeling happy, simply because your body is too fatigued to be happy or jolly. Tiredness is such an underestimated thing.

Then there are headaches (which I am now told may be migraines), sickness and nausea. I don't know if these are just things that come hand in hand with tiredness and fatigue. I have seen many doctors and no one can tell me the answer to this. The standard reply was, "your blood work looks ok, I can't see any reason for this." They cannot see beyond the blood results and the fact I have cystinosis. In their eyes if the blood results are ok I must be ok. They are unwilling to look into extensions of cystinosis. It has taken me 10 years to get my headaches looked into. It was not one of my London doctors, my kidney doctor, my eye doctor or my gastroenterologist that decided to look into my headaches and give me a scan. It was my ENT doctor when I went for my hearing test. I told him how I always had headaches and that none of my doctors seem to be listening. He sent me for an MRI scan. He listened to me and he tried to help me and I'm so grateful to him. The scan showed some tiny white dots and I was referred to a neurologist. He assured me that they are nothing to worry about but started me on some migraine medication, one of which also helped my tummy so much better than any meds any other doctor had given me. The gastroenterologist even discharged me saying there was nothing more he could do despite the fact I clearly was not well.

Cystinosis is not all bad but I wanted to be honest about how it affects me. I don't see the point in sugar coating things, but surprisingly there are a number of good things too.

Having cystinosis makes you stronger. It makes you realise what really matters and learn to let go of the things that don't. I don't hold on to silly arguments, my mum always taught me to choose my battles and that the most important thing in life is to be happy and to try your best. If you have put in 100% effort, there is nothing more you can do. We all have bad days, even people without cystinosis do, so if it all goes wrong just let it go and start fresh tomorrow. If something will only make a small difference but it will impact on your life greatly you need to weigh up whether it will really be worth it. I feel sometimes doctors need reminding that we are not just blood results, we have lives and feelings. Don't be afraid to ask for advice. Cystinosis is rare; doctors don't always get it right. Ask around on the cystinosis Facebook page or on the Cystinosis Foundation page.

You can't deal with cystinosis on your own, especially when first diagnosed. It's a lot to manage, don't be afraid to admit you're struggling and ask a family member to look after your child so that you can have a break. Don't be too hard on yourself. My mum said when she first got me home she was terrified she would measure my meds wrong or miss a dose. Mum said there were times I was so sick I could not keep my meds down no matter how many times I tried. In the end the doctor told her to give my tummy a rest and start again in the morning.

Cystinosis has made me a stronger person and I try not to worry about things that are out of my control. I have an appointment to talk about dialysis options soon and this really scares me. But it's not for another month and if I dwell on it I will go crazy, what will be will be and when it happens I will find strength I never knew I had.

I can normally see the good in everyone and try to see both sides of a story. I have also met so many people that I would not have met otherwise. At the cystinosis conferences I have met many lovely people from all over the world. Cystinosis is what made me have the strength to start traveling and meeting people in the first place.

My life with cystinosis has, at times, been met with a lot of adversity, which a lot of people would presume no longer existed in today's world. The truth is though today's world is a lot better, you will never completely rid the world of adversity when there is still so much that people do not want to understand or is not common. For instance: A GP practice has refused to register me with them in the past because the cost of my medication was too high.

I was refused entry to a level 3 qualification because the leader of the course said I was not able and that the course was for people who were able to take more responsibility. I had a meeting with the leader, a Shaw Trust adviser and an equality officer. After some discussion and time the leader could not find a good enough reason to refuse me and I was allowed to continue on the level 3 course, which I have since passed!

I have been told after a job interview that I was not successful because they felt my condition would stop me from putting enough energy into the job.

At school I did not have many friends and children would often refuse to sit next to me because of the smell of Cystagon and children would not touch my books or belongings. I do not feel angry at the children for this. My mum said that children cannot accept things that they do not understand. I do feel that the teachers accepted this as normal after a few years and gave up trying to resolve the issue.

In secondary school a teaching assistant took me to the side and asked me if I minded keeping a lavender tissue on my desk as she did not like the smell of Cystagon.

She also asked me if I had tried wearing perfume! Anybody who has handled Cystagon knows that you can wear all the perfume you like the Cystagon will still come through. I did have some tablets to try to help with the smell but I struggled taking all my tablets as it was, without adding more to the mix, and they didn't really work that well. I did not tell my parents or anyone about this incident as I was far too embarrassed.

A secondary school teacher once lost my homework and when I tried to tell her I had handed it in she argued with me and said, "If you did not have so much time off school you would be able to do your homework." The whole class laughed, and I wanted to cry, as the only reason I had so much time off was because I was either sick or at the hospital. The next day the teacher came to me and said she found my homework. She did not even apologize for losing it or the things she said.

By far the worst thing, that still upsets me even now, is when I tried to do a beauty therapy course at college. I was only about 3 months into the course when a teacher asked to have a meeting with me and my mum. In this meeting she said I could continue my course but I WOULD fail because of the smell of my Cystagon. This was because I had to practice on my class and no one in the class wanted me to work with them. Also shortly before this when they advertised reduced cost trials to the public the client who came refused to work with me. I believe however that the client was told about the smell before meeting me as I heard her say to my tutor that she did not think the smell would be as strong. They did not ask my permission to do this.

In the meeting with the tutors they suggested I do not work with people and asked if I had considered working in floristry instead, where I would not have much contact with people. At this point both I and my mum were very angry and crying. What they did not know was my mum is a florist and has worked in a flower shop for years. Mum told them that actually as a florist you have to be able to work closely with people especially for events such as funerals. They then took me down to the careers advisor to look at what else I could do. I was completely heart-broken, especially when they suggested I should not work with people. My mum was so upset she called a lawyer for advice. The lawyer said that because they said I could do the course but that I would fail because of the smell it was not against the law. It would only have been against the law if they said I could not do the course at all. This was a few years ago now, it is possible the law has changed or that he was not correct. I have no idea but we were too tired and upset to pursue it. I did however stay on the course for another few weeks despite being heartbroken at the way they treated me. I'm a very stubborn person and I was going to make them have to talk to me every day. I was not going to let them push me out. However, after a few weeks I did leave.

Every hurdle in my life however, has always had some sort of silver lining. I went to a new special training college a few hours away. I had to live in a dormitory down there and only come home every other weekend, which was a little scary to start with. In the end this turned out to be one of the best times of my life. I made a lot of friends there, and no one even mentioned the smell of my meds. At first this felt really surreal to me and I was very nervous to get too involved with social activities or people, but after a while I had a lot of friends and really enjoyed myself, so much I didn't want to leave. I got an extension on my course and stayed there about a year. Unfortunately its funding was reduced and I don't believe it offers the same facilities any more. Courses and budgets were being reduced while I was there and there was talk of moving to a cheaper venue. I now know they have moved. This place was my saviour. It taught me that the way I was treated was not normal, it gave me the confidence to socialise and have the normal experiences and enjoy life like any other girl my age (which was around 17/18 at the time). It taught me not to just accept things and that I have the same rights as anybody else.

Like I said I am now 28. I have a lot more hurdles to overcome, but I have a job in a school and I am level 3 qualified. I have a house and live with my partner and retired greyhound. I still struggle a little socially, but I have an amazing loving family and have achieved so much more than I ever thought I could.

Follow Kayla's blog at www.lemonsoflife.co.uk

Kayla's Father's Story

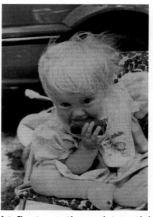

When Kayla was born she seemed perfectly normal and indeed for the first 18 months everything seemed to be going well. She reached her normal milestones well on time, she was quite intelligent and was eating and drinking well. She first stood up at about 15 months, her coordination was good and could talk well for her age. Then age about 16 months we noticed that she had become reluctant to eat. At first we thought nothing of this assuming that it was just a phase she was going through. We had also noticed that she was somewhat smaller than other babies of the same age, which perhaps to be expected as her mother was only 5 feet tall.

It is also worthy of note that by now we had noticed, but were not concerned about the fact, that when Kayla was born she was dark haired and by now she was extremely fair haired.

The month of May was very long for us. We had just bought a new house and had to contend with all of those moving in problems. After the house move we became concerned that her progress with walking seemed to have stopped. We, naturally, took her to see the family doctor whom could find nothing wrong, so he referred us to the pediatrician at our local hospital, whom also could find nothing wrong, and it was decided that Kayla would just be a late walker. Another 3-4 weeks passed and by now we were seriously concerned about Kayla's eating. She was eating literally nothing at all, not even sweets and chocolate. Instead she started to drink two or more pints of milk at night, which also meant she was waking every half an hour or so to have her bottle filled.

So it was back to the doctors. Again he could find nothing wrong but this time he arranged for Kayla to have some blood tests, once more, nothing was to be found. We were sent back home and told to stop her milk at night in an attempt to make her hungry. Three days later we had a phone call from our babysitter saying that by now Kayla was so weak that she could not even stand up. Once again we went back to our doctor. We were immediately sent back to the pediatrician, whom could still find nothing wrong even with more blood tests, but he agreed to admit her into the ward so that she could be observed more closely. It was difficult to convince the doctors that Kayla was eating absolutely nothing at all and the pediatrician led us to believe that it was just her stubbornness and that she would just have to be force fed in order to overcome it.

Kayla was admitted on the Monday and by Tuesday evening they agreed that she was not eating and by now she was weighing less than she was at 11 or 12 months of age. Wednesday evening doctors told us that they thought Kayla had a kidney problem but they would need to carry out more tests to be sure and they would see us again on Friday morning.

By now, having been told that it was just Kayla's stubbornness, we were quite taken back by this bad news, but worse was to come. Friday came and the pediatrician told us that he was not sure but he thought Kayla had an extremely rare condition by the name of cystinosis and that this would have to be confirmed by a pediatric specialist. He attempted to explain to us about the condition and what it would involve, but it was all too much to take in at one time. Over the weekend work was to start on the correction of her newly discovered chemical deficiencies, which we were told would be very difficult and possibly beyond the capabilities of that hospital.

By the following Monday Kayla was stable and supposedly responding to treatment. On leaving the ward on Tuesday evening we expressed concern over the fact that Kayla would not stop crying and both of her hands were constantly clenched. This was actually (although unknown at the time) the beginning of the most frightening episode to date. The next day we were both called from work urgently and when we arrived at the hospital we found Kayla in the emergency treatment room wired up to various machines with several doctors in attendance having what appeared to be some sort of muscular spasm which was extremely disturbing to watch.

Fortunately the doctors were able to get the better of this attack in 20 minutes or so. We now know that this was an attack of tetany caused mainly by a very low calcium level, which in turn was caused by the doctors playing around with Kayla's metabolism. If the calcium level falls dangerously below normal hypocalcemia is induced which very rapidly causes the heart to race away due to increased neuromuscular activity, and rapidly causing tetany to progress to cardiac and respiratory arrest. On Thursday evening Kayla suffered a severe and nearly fatal attack of hypocalcemia, which was extremely distressing and frightening to watch. It seemed to take forever for Kayla to overcome this, at times Kayla's heart beat exceeded 230 bpm and I am led to believe by doctors that the average child heart can take a maximum of only 240 bpm.

I think this was the last straw for our local hospital, admitting that they did not really have the knowledge to deal with this, and, from this point on Kayla received permanent doctor attendance as if they were waiting for something to happen. Kayla received this permanent attendance up to and during her rapid transfer to London hospital early the following Friday morning. My wife travelled in the ambulance whilst I followed in the car, easier said than done in Central London traffic.

At London hospital there is a specialist in cystinosis by the name of Dr. William Van't Hoff, pediatric registrar (now Consultant Pediatric Nephrologist at Great Ormond Street Hospital and is currently Joint Interim Theme Director for the NIHR Clinical Research Network: Division 3.) whom has given us a much better understanding of Kayla's condition. So in six months we have gone from what we thought was a perfectly normal healthy baby to a very ill baby indeed.

Something which annoyed me very much at the time and still annoys me now is the fact that it took so long to convince the doctors that there was something wrong with Kayla. They just did not believe that she was not eating a thing and they even told us initially to stop giving her sweets and chocolate in an attempt to get her to eat proper food, but this was the point she was not even eating sweets.

Dr. Van't Hoff confirmed within about 3-4 hours of arriving at London Hospital that Kayla did in fact have cystinosis and over the next two weeks was able to give us a much better understanding of the condition. My wife and I were both totally devastated when the first thing Dr. Van't Hoff wished us to understand was the fact that there is absolutely no cure for the condition at all and all that could be offered was medication to ease Kayla through the rest of her life.

Dr. Van't Hoff was very interested in Kayla as she was only the 67th person to have the condition and survive in the UK. Until the mid-70s if you were born with cystinosis (which was not known about then) it was normal for you to die before reaching your teens. So for this reason the oldest surviving sufferer in this country was only 18 (now approximately 51 years of age).

Initially upon being told this we assumed that Kayla would die at an early age, but we misunderstood. Although he admitted that very little was known about cystinosis still, and he would not commit himself either, Dr. Van't Hoff could not see why, that with appropriate medication, Kayla could not lead a virtually normal and full life.

Back At Home
Kayla came home after several touch and go weeks. Day to day living was sometimes quite a traumatic experience for Kayla. The main problem for Kayla, and us, being the administration of her large quantity of medicines and drugs; Kayla needed between 15 and 25 doses of medicine and drugs some between 4, 6 and 12 hours every single day.

Kayla had the bulk of her medicine in three batches per day, early morning, noon and night as most of them dissolved in water. The problem there was trying to get Kayla to drink her now bitterly tainted water well before her next batch was due. This was normally accomplished by a great deal of deceit and trickery, much as telling Kayla that the drink was something which it was not. If the batch was not drunk in time, the next batch had to be postponed and it could take a day or two to get back on schedule again.

The relatively short time between some doses meant that all of her medication had to go with her. Her medication needed to be portable because if we went out anywhere we could not guarantee to get home in time for the next batch as you never know when you are going to be involved in a breakdown or accident, so they were always to hand unless we were literally within walking distance to home.

Probably the biggest problem with medication administration was the drug cysteamine. The cysteamine was given to Kayla by both my wife and I as it was such a problem and would therefore be unfair to ask the babysitter to give it. Cysteamine, as mentioned earlier, has an extremely foul taste and leaves a very foul smell on your breath, best described as being similar to boiled cabbage for several hours afterwards. For this reason Kayla obviously wanted nothing to do with it at all, but she had to have it, so we had to force it down her. It often took two of us to give it. Accompanied with the loud screams and crying it did seem almost cruel at first but it had to be done. As if this was not bad enough, Kayla was sometimes sick between 20 minutes to an hour after administration (the main side effect).

As already mentioned the doses and drugs varied on a weekly basis, and to decide the dose and frequency required Kayla had to attend hospital on a weekly or fortnightly basis depending on her present stability to have an electrolyte blood test. This was also quite distressing for Kayla but, once again, it was necessary. Also, to decide the cysteamine dose Kayla needed to attend Guy's Hospital on a monthly to three monthly basis, depending on her present stability as only Guy's had the means and equipment to test for cystine levels. This was a big inconvenience for the family as it involved a day off work and a day's traveling to and across London and back not to mention the expense.

One of the other major problems with Kayla's condition was the constant wetting. Kayla used between 10 - 15 nappies in any one day, and during the night she would completely soak her bed and pillow. This meant constant daily washing of the bed clothes, pillows, clothes and nappies, which added greatly to our daily workload, bearing in mind that both my wife and I worked full time.

Other side effects, again previously mentioned, had greatly affected her height and weight. Kayla, at age 2 years, weighed 18lbs and stood at 71.5 cm. The average height and weight for a two year old is approximately 28lbs and 98cm. So you can see that in just her first two years Kayla was already well behind the average child in this respect. The only improvement she'd had in regards to physical appearance was that once treatment began, Kayla's hair very slightly started to regain color, mainly on the sides and back.

We also had to be wary of any falls that Kayla had as she was more likely than other children to do serious damage to herself, having, "the bones of an old age pensioner," although we were hopeful that her bone structure would improve.

We had been told repeatedly that the only way that we were going to get Kayla to grow to any size at all was to try get her to eat, and that was by far the hardest task to accomplish. Kayla was given extra vitamins and Maxijul (calorie substitute), but there was no substitute for real food and all that it contained and so we encouraged Kayla to eat as much as possible. It was a desperately emotional battle. We and the babysitter were constantly trying to tempt her to eat. Occasionally we tempted her to eat maybe just half a small tin of tomato soup but it often come back up again.

There was also yet another inconvenience, this time related to research. Due to the rarity of Kayla's condition there was quite a lot of interest in Kayla; both from qualified experienced doctors, and from junior trainee doctors. As a result, whilst at Guy's we were visited by two trainee doctors whom wished to base part of their study on Kayla. This meant having to explain the case history of Kayla from the very beginning right up to date each time. It also meant more prods and pokes for Kayla and yet more questions for us to have to answer. Also whilst at Guy's we took part in a survey to help assess the effectiveness of giving cysteamine. This survey was voluntary and we had to sign a disclaimer in case harm occurred or any mistakes were made. The test lasted for 48 hours during which time Kayla was subject to about 40 injections and blood test at regular intervals throughout the day and night. This was in addition to her normal treatment.

This was extremely traumatic for Kayla and we were beginning to wonder if it would not have a lasting mental effect on her, being woken up several times in the night just to have a blood test and all. Later when back at home we still received calls from our local hospital asking if we would be kind enough to bring Kayla along to take part in 5th year medical student exams. It meant even more time off work, etc., etc.

Although it was a real inconvenience we felt we must oblige as it was only through research and new doctors that more effective treatment and maybe even one day a cure could be found. So, until that day comes I, my wife and Kayla will just have to grin and bear it.

WHAT'S THE PRICE FOR A CURE?
By Bill Kunde

I heard the question asked, "What is the price of a cure for cystinosis?" One must first calculate the cost of this chronic disease.

What is the cost of thousands of lives lost to cystinosis? How many novels were never written? How many melodies never composed? How many songs never sung, and life changing research never begun?

What is the cost of a kiss never given again, a hug never felt again, laughter never heard again? What is the cost of the loss of the milestones in the life never realized, graduations, weddings, births and anniversaries?

What is the cost of endless needle sticks, doctor and hospital visits, unrelenting medication schedules, stomach aches, eye pain, muscle weakness, swallowing difficulties, poor growth, vomiting, and fatigue?

What is the cost of constant worry about the future? Is tomorrow going to bring another challenge for the one I love and how do we overcome it once again? The cost of the anxiety of waiting for the next blood values? Does more medication need to be added? Are the doses going to be adjusted again? Are we staying ahead of the disease progression or are we falling behind?

So you see the cost is unmeasurable. It's paid for in heartache and tears and will be continued to be paid until a cure is found. The price of a cure, simply put is **PRICELESS**.

The art selections included on the

following pages are part of the

Cystinosis Research Network's

Dream, Achieve, Inspire

art exhibit.

The entire exhibit collection can be viewed at
http://dreamachieveinspire.org

"Happy Home"
By Yuankang Ma, China

"Courage"
By Stephanie Trudell, Nebraska, USA

The entire exhibit collection can be viewed at
http://dreamachieveinspire.org

"Mask"
By Trati Vilarino deUriarte, Spain

"Fun and Playful"
By Lilian Esther Gonzalez, Martinez, Venezuela

The entire exhibit collection can be viewed at
http://dreamachieveinspire.org

"Sevgi (love)"
By Sistinozis Ailesiyiz, Turkey

"Peaceful Hope"
By Hariharan S.V., India

The entire exhibit collection can be viewed at
http://dreamachieveinspire.org

"Happy Hippos"
By Santi Mortimer, Ibanez, Valencia, Spain

"Good and Evil Annie"
By Annie Kwakkel, The Netherlands

The entire exhibit collection can be viewed at
http://dreamachieveinspire.org

"My Three Worlds"
By Amanda Leigh, New York, USA

"Power"
By Daniel da Silva Lima, Brazil

The entire exhibit collection can be viewed at
http://dreamachieveinspire.org

"Spring"
By Hana Ahmed, Cairo, Egypt

"Geode Number One"
By Lee Knaus, Florida, USA

The entire exhibit collection can be viewed at
http://dreamachieveinspire.org

"Two Fish"
By Livia Grace Stilke
December 19, 2005 – September 26, 2014

The entire exhibit collection can be viewed at
http://dreamachieveinspire.org

Kenzie's Story
By Peggy Kunde

As our little angel Kenzie started the miracle of life she was small. Over time we became concerned with her not eating well, vomiting, not growing, being fussy and constantly changing diapers. The doctor noticed her legs were bowed. She was diagnosed with Hypophosphatemic Rickets. Kenzie was still not improving, her mom, Katie, decided she would put all of Kenzie's symptoms in the computer to figure out what was going on with Kenzie's little body. She told me what she came up with and cystinosis was among the list. I said, "No, Kenzie doesn't have that."

As she was getting sicker and ended up in the hospital it was time for the doctors to figure it out. At two years old, we received our answer.

This tiny little girl was getting weaker and weaker. Then a few days before Christmas we were told it was cystinosis. There were so many questions going through our minds. What do we do? Where do we go? What challenges will we be going through? How do we make our little angel better? We were devastated.

I knew I would eventually be strong, but it was very hard until we understood what this disease does and what needed to be done. We knew we had to be strong for Katie and Shawn. Katie surprises me at how strong of a mom she is, and I am there for her whenever she needs me.

Every day we struggle with eye drops and medication, but it's part of our daily routine. I still have sad days when Kenzie just isn't herself. She seems to always have a smile and shows her silly sense of humor. Always asking, "WHY?"

Kenzie's big sister, Brielle, struggled with what was going on, but as she watches what Kenzie goes through on a daily basis, she knows Kenzie needs a little more attention. Brielle is the BEST big sister ever. Brielle is also Kenzie's protector when we aren't looking.

At four years of age Kenzie has the biggest heart. She is the one who gets me through my tough days. She doesn't want to be treated like a baby. Because of her small stature some people treat her that way, but when she talks they are amazed at what she has to say. She tells you what she thinks. I love that she is so honest.

As the weather gets nicer Kenzie struggles with the warm weather and I struggle because she can't enjoy activities outside for long periods of time. She has a hard time with regulating her body temperature. Drinking water and a cool spot usually help. For a long time I didn't realize they had a hard time sweating, or rather, they don't sweat.

Nancy Stack was our greatest inspiration. Just talking with her I knew I would have a long journey with my granddaughter. We have hope and faith that a cure is found for our cystinosis family. Even though it is not the rare disease I would pick, it's the best of diseases with such an awesome network of research and families.

Advice from an Expert...
Living with a Weird Disease
by Sarah Larimore, 11 years old

1. Go to conferences. Everyone has buttons and sunglasses and somebody always throws up. It's great!

2. Dogs are awesome. You should get one

3. Taking meds is rotten. Just do it and get it over with

4. When you are in the hospital be nice to nurses, then you get popsicles

5. You should always wear the color yellow because it will brighten your day

6. The beach is the best place ever. Find one and go there many times

7. Real friends don't care about medicine breathe

8. When you don't feel like eating, get Mexican food with chips and salsa

9. Do what the doctor tells you, even if he looks funny.

10. Never, ever, ever give up. Ever.

Life Story
By Mack Maxwell

Early Life and the Cystinosis Diagnosis

I was born on April 9, 1964. My infant years were normal, except for photophobia. I can remember photophobia since I was 4 years old. At age 6, while in first grade, my slow growth became very noticeable to me. I was about a head shorter than other classmates at the time. It took a long time to determine a correct diagnosis in the early 70's. Several doctors misdiagnosed my condition as diabetes. Our family doctor and friend, Dr. Percy Cook was determined to find somebody that could correctly diagnose and treat me.

Finally, at approximately 8 years of age, doctors in Fort Worth, TX suspected that I might have infantile nephropathic cystinosis. Doctors in Fort Worth referred me to Dr. Harrison in Baltimore, MD and he confirmed the infantile nephropathic cystinosis diagnosis. Dr. Harrison did an excellent job in treating me and informed us that an eventual kidney transplant would be necessary. This was very exciting because my instincts told me that the kidney transplant would make me feel healthy and change my life forever!

Cystinosis - Kidney Transplant

My opportunity of having a chance at the perfect kidney transplant happened in 1975. Since I was adopted, this could have made the process difficult, but it did not. Lynne Blissit, my biological mother was contacted and without hesitation offered to give me one of her kidneys. Fortunately, I only had to go through 3 weeks of dialysis before my transplant. At the time of transplant, at age 11, I was 3'11 and 39 lbs. The kidney transplant was performed on June 10, 1975 by Dr. Paul Peters in Dallas, TX at Parkland Hospital. As an adult, I'm 5'3" and 135 lbs. As of this writing in April 2016, I've had my transplanted kidney for just over 40 years 10 months. My kidney is in great shape as evidenced by my 0.90 creatinine.

Cystinosis - Eyes
After my transplant, I felt great except for my eyes. I was told that it was very unlikely anything could ever be done about my eye condition. Somehow, I intuitively knew this was incorrect, but I feared that the solution to this issue may come around age 70. For years, I had severe photophobia and eye pain that got worse with age. Many times it would feel like sand was in my eyes. Fortunately in June 1999, at age 35, while doing a yahoo internet search, I discovered there was a cystinosis treatment available for my eyes at the National Institutes of Health (NIH). My first visit to the NIH was in September 1999. This was my first time to meet with Dr. Gahl and Dr. Kaiser. Dr. Kaiser gave me Cysteamine eyedrops which instantly eliminated my pain and changed my life. One year later, my eyes were completely crystal free and have been ever since.

Cystinosis – Cystagon and Procysbi
During my September, 1999 visit to the NIH, Dr. Gahl put me on Cystagon in order to minimize future damage from cystinosis. Taking Cystagon was a huge challenge because of the severe side effects. The stomach issues

were the most difficult for me. I struggled taking Cystagon and did the best that I could.

On April 30, 2013, Procysbi, a new form of Cysteamine drug that eliminated crystals became FDA approved. I was a test subject on the Procysbi drug trial in 2012 and have been taking it ever since. Since taking Procysbi, I do not have the side effect of stomach issues anymore! Procysbi has been a real game changer for me!

Cystinosis – Sleep Apnea
The most recent cystinosis event that I've encountered is my 2003 diagnosis of sleep apnea. Sleep apnea has been more of an inconvenience than a challenge. Nightly use of a Bi-Pap machine has been excellent treatment for me.

Education
I graduated from Mansfield High School in Mansfield, TX in May, 1982. I graduated from the University of Texas at Arlington with a Bachelor of Science in Information Systems in August, 1986.

Employment
I've worked in the Information Technology field for my entire professional career. I started my first professional job for Tarrant County College (TCC) on November 17, 1986 at age 22. For about the first 11 years at TCC, I was a COBOL and CICS programmer.

In 1997, I left TCC, in order to pursue the Y2K opportunity with The Sabre Group (TSG). This opportunity gave me a chance to make more money and to have stand-by flight privileges with American Airlines. The majority of my work was doing COBOL programming on an AS400 computer during my time with Sabre.

On August 31, 1999 I left Sabre due to a large company wide layoff. Fortunately, I was able to get my old job back almost immediately. On October 4, 1999 I returned back to TCC. I continued working as a COBOL programmer until TCC eliminated the mainframe computer around 2002. I've worked several years with the Desktop Support team. As of 2015, I've been working with the Application Services team.

Cystinosis Conferences
It was because of a yahoo internet search in 1999 that I started to find out more about Cystinosis. I learned about a conference in San Diego, CA in August, 1999. At age 35, this was the first time that I had ever met another person that had cystinosis. This was the first time that I learned about the current and ongoing research in cystinosis. This was to be just the beginning of many conferences that I would attend.

I enjoy keeping up with my friends in the cystinosis community. I've attended most of the American conferences since 1999 and had the opportunity to attend several European cystinosis conferences. The European conferences have given me the opportunity to visit Amsterdam, Barcelona, Paris, Dublin, Prague, Venice, Manchester, and south west Scotland.

Being one of the oldest persons with cystinosis, I try to offer some advice. The most important advice that I can give is the importance of exercise. I've had the opportunity to speak about this at conferences a number of times throughout the years.

Interests and Hobbies

My personal interests include sports, working out, trying out new restaurants, Texas Hold'em Poker tournaments, and travel.

I'm a sports fan and I especially love football. I've been a huge Dallas Cowboys fan since 1970 when I was only 6 years old. I had the opportunity to meet Roger Staubach in 1975 just a few months before my kidney transplant. In 2005, my Mother and I got to meet with Roger Staubach again for a 30 year reunion!

For baseball, I'm a Texas Rangers fan and I enjoy attending a few games during the year. I even got to attend a couple of World Series games when the Texas Rangers finally made the World Series in 2010 and 2011.

I started working out in off-season football in the 7th grade at the age of 12. This is when I learned the importance of physical fitness. During the years, some of my sports have included playing baseball and softball, basketball, running 5Ks, and running/walking 2 Half Marathons.

I've been playing Texas Hold'em Poker Tournaments since 2005. It's been a fun hobby and I've had some success. I've played international Texas Hold'em Poker Tournaments in Rio de Janeiro, Brazil and in Dublin, Ireland. I've cashed in one WSOP tournament at Choctaw Casino in Durant, Oklahoma.

From a very early age, I've always loved to travel. My Dad was a mechanic for American Airlines and we got to fly a lot. I fondly remember several trips to San Diego to visit family and a couple of nice trips to Hawaii. Even though we could fly, my Dad really preferred camping and going in the motorhome. We've camped in most of Texas and Arkansas. My favorite camping vacation was a week in the Smoky Mountains. As an adult, my favorite travel destinations are Brazil, Europe, and Las Vegas.

My Story
Whitney McElroy

To put my thoughts and ideas down on paper doesn't really seem to do "my story" justice. I have tried to come up with the appropriate words to describe how totally crazy "my story" is, and over and over again, I am left speechless or wordless. There simply are no words to describe the magnitude of the blessing, miracle, or gift that my twins truly are.

On September 9th, 2016, I gave birth to boy/girl twins, Kaiden and Lila. They were born early at 30 weeks, which actually is not that early for twins. They were small but strong, tiny but fighters, like me, their mama. Kaiden weighed 2 pounds, 5 ounces and Lila weighed 2 pounds, 10 ounces. They spent 6 weeks in the NICU not due to any major health issues but due to their small size. The hospital would not let them come home until they were at least 4 pounds. Kaiden and Lila were born breathing on their own, which is rare for twins born at 30 weeks. They only got oxygen for a few days to strengthen their bronchioles, not to help them breathe. I learned, during my twins' stay in the NICU, that many twins are born at 1 pound and frequently one twin passes away while the other survives.

Why is this all so miraculous you ask? Why is "my story" different than any other twin moms story? Well the answer is because me, their mama, wasn't supposed to live to see my 10th birthday.

In 1980 I was diagnosed with cystinosis, a rare metabolic disorder that was supposed to take my life by my 10th birthday! It took many months and hospital stays for my parents to get a proper diagnosis for my illness due to the rarity of the disease. After searching for an answer to my symptoms, my parents were given a grim prognosis. I was diagnosed with cystinosis at Shands Teaching Hospital, which is part of the University of Florida. Doctors told my parents that I would need a kidney transplant by age 9, be 3 feet tall and likely not live to see my 10th birthday!

My parents refused to let that dismal prognosis discourage them from doing any and everything to keep me alive and thriving. They made the difficult decision to put me on an experimental medication used to treat cystinosis. I have remained on a form of that medication (cysteamine) for the last 35 years and it has proven to be a lifesaving treatment. I ended up not needing a kidney transplant until 2011 at the age of 33. My mom donated a kidney to me.

Being a mother was something that I had dreamed of since I was as young as I can remember. Having cystinosis really, or so I thought, complicated that dream. Having a baby post- transplant is risky for both the mother and the baby however I was willing to take the risk to become a mom. After having a miscarriage in October 2014 I felt like the likelihood of my dream coming true was becoming farther and farther out of reach. I pretty much gave up at that point and my husband and I had other major life changes to deal with including the unexpected death of his dad, my father in law.

I continued to pray for a baby knowing that at the age of 36 my dream was fading away. I was pleasantly surprised to find out I was pregnant in March of 2015 and blown away to find out it was twins! When the ultrasound tech showed me the two heartbeats I really did not believe what I saw. I was certain something would go wrong and that I would lose one or both babies. I was very secretive about the pregnancy, mainly out of fear, and didn't even tell my parents until May. I was terrified and elated all at the same time. I knew how risky it was to carry twins after a kidney transplant and the first time I went to the perinatologist (high risk OB) I was certain she would advise me to end the pregnancy or reduce it to one baby.

To my surprise she did not! She was extremely optimistic with me and said I was as "healthy" as a post kidney transplant patient could be and should plan on delivering two healthy babies. My pregnancy was not easy and was filled with constant doctor appointments, blood draws, tests, etc. On a typical week I was at the doctor 1-2 times a week for the remainder of the pregnancy (12-30 weeks). In the end, I had the babies about a month before we had planned to have the C-section due to the sudden onset of high blood pressure that was becoming pre-eclampsia and HELLP syndrome. The babies spent 42 days in the NICU but were healthy and breathing on their own at birth. Their only issue was low birth weight.

Lila and Kaiden are absolute and complete miracles. When they were born I knew that they were given to me by a higher being. They have shown me that truly, we are not in control of our own lives. I cannot express what they mean to me and I don't know what I did to deserve them. Perhaps, they were given to me to help inspire others who have cystinosis or other incurable diseases. I have worked hard to overcome obstacles that the disease has caused me and I have also worked endlessly to keep myself as healthy as possible. Perhaps Lila and Kaiden were given to me to show others that you can live a "normal" life even after an unfavorable medical diagnosis.

Becoming a mom to boy/girl twins has by far been the most rewarding event in my life. No one though, prepared me for the exhaustion I would face when caring for them (and working full time as a speech therapist). I constantly have to remind myself how blessed and lucky I am to have them, especially when my patience is fading and all I really want is a nap and a hot shower. Almost daily, I hear or read of stories about a mom who lost a baby (frequently a twin) due to prematurity or other medical issues at birth or shortly thereafter. It happens all the time!

Raising twins when you have a chronic illness is the hardest thing I have ever done but again, I am blessed to get to do it, and beyond thankful that I have been given this experience. That is what keeps me going.

There is Joy in the Journey: Our Story
By Katie Monaghan

Our story is like so many others.

We were new parents, but we felt there was something more going on. As new parents, with worries about your baby vomiting and peeing a lot, our concerns didn't go far. Until she stopped growing and then began to lose weight. It took about 6 months, with numerous doctor visits, specialist referrals, multiple tests and hospital stays to get a diagnosis. But, it came.

At the age of 18 months, in the fall of 2007, Abbi was diagnosed with Fanconi syndrome and cystinosis.

In the middle of all this, Terry, Abbi's father and my husband, was diagnosed with a heart condition that, eventually, was easily fixed. However, there were episodes occurring at that time that could have been fatal.

I felt that I was at a loss, and that I was in the middle. I feared that I was about to lose it all. It seemed that Abbi was fading away and we were also distressed about Terry's recent diagnosis.

As I look back on that time, there are times that are engraved in my memory, and still give me a nauseous feeling when I think about them. Mostly, we lived in a fog. We had, and still have, a lot of support that has gotten us through some tough times. For the first few years, I really have no idea how we managed. People somehow thought that we had it all together.

There is no handbook on raising a child with a rare chronic disease. So, we kind of make it up as we go along. We get a ton of advice; some is great, and some, we simply smile and nod at. What has worked for our family is humor, balance and making quality of life so very important!

It took some time, but we got out of the fog and found our groove. I still have moments where I feel stuck. Sometimes these moments pass quickly, and sometimes they drag me down for weeks on end. However, I am learning to deal with them in a better way by changing the negative thoughts with positive ones.

Abbi is a bright, energetic, creative little lady. Living a "normal" life myself, and then watching everything that she goes through to live her life... it can be easy and it can also drag you down. Abbi is resilient, like most kids. She adapts to her surroundings and makes life work.

Abbi has learned how at address negative comments about her small size. She is able to keep up with her friends in active play by having a few tricks up her sleeve. She participates in all of the physical activities at school, with a little tweaking here and there. She has amazing self-confidence, she takes pride in her work, and she is kind and generous to others. Abbi has goals and dreams for the future and I now have no doubts that these are all achievable.

Cystinosis is not something you would ever wish upon anyone. It can be all-consuming with around the clock medication, procedures and appointments. But, it also has changed and continues to change how we live, feel and love. I appreciate things I never thought of before. We live in the moment. It has helped me to have great empathy in my job and to not judge others.

It took some time and a few drafts to figure out what I was going to write or how I was going to write it. From day to day, things are always so different, based on how I feel and look at our journey. There is still so much to come with fears and triumphs. But cystinosis has not broken us. It has actually made us stronger as a family.

Just the other night, we were all lying in bed (the 4 of us, Terry, Abbi, her brother William, and myself) with the window open. We could hear the birds chirping and the sounds of people walking nearby and cars driving by. We talked, we giggled, we all snuggled and I had so much joy in my heart. All I could think was, "is there anything more you even need in life than this?"

A Very Sincere Thank You
By Clinton Moore

Our story starts in much the same way as many other cystinosis families. Everything at birth was normal and soon we were settled back at home with a tiny baby adjusting to our new life. But like many of the cystinosis beginnings, it was about to change. When my son, Chandler, turned about 10 months old we began to notice he had a thirst that could not be quenched. When you held him near the kitchen sink he would literally throw himself at it, as he knew that's where the water was. He would guzzle it like I have never seen. We immediately called his pediatrician. She ordered labs and then it was a waiting game for the results. When the tests came back she called and informed us we needed to head to the only children's hospital in Delaware, A.I.Dupont Hospital for Children.

In the days to come it was a steady flow of doctors and nurses trying desperately to put the pieces together. Seemed like hourly they wanted more blood or were taking us off to another test. Day after day it continued, lots of people, but no answers. After 9 long days a "suspected" diagnosis had been finally made but, we would have to be transported to another children's hospital in Pennsylvania for confirmation. Two weeks later it was confirmed. Chandler had cystinosis.

Once back home and adjusting to our "new" normal we began our own research of what cystinosis was. The Internet can be a place full of knowledge and explanation, but can also fuel fears and worries. We learned all the do's and dont's of this illness and what to expect in the coming years. We learned of experimental treatments for corneal crystals and the history of cysteamine.

We also learned that there were several advocacy groups already established doing wonderful things. These groups seemed to have everything covered from fundraising, to raising awareness, to funding research. We read many stories from other families that were involved in these groups and I honestly didn't think I needed to do anything as they were already doing so much. I knew I couldn't make a difference as I am only one person and my comfort zone really isn't much larger than your average cookie. So for the next 8 years I did nothing but treat my son and kept faith that all the ones that were involved in the battle against cystinosis would continue. I really thought that all that could be done for cystinosis was already being done. So why get involved?

Over this time period I continued reading stories of families who were holding fundraisers. Certainly not something I had ever attempted before but I found myself constantly thinking maybe I should. I really doubted that I could pull it off or raise very much money. Little did we know that Chandler had been overhearing our conversations and told us that we should try because we were already doing a small event at our home every

Christmas anyway. So the next thing we knew we were planning our first ever cystinosis fundraiser.

During the last few weeks before this event I found myself frantically handing out flyers to anyone who was willing to take one. I hung them in store windows, left them on counters, even had them on our local news. I so wanted it to be a success and it turned out to be just that, but not in a way that I thought.

You see, our particular fundraiser has a lot of moving parts, a lot of details, requires many hours of planning, and also brings a lot of stress. I actually convinced myself that this would be my first, and my last. That was until my phone rang...

The lady on the other end of the call had many questions, and even though she never came out and said it, she had me convinced that she wanted to donate. She requested we meet at her home a few hours later and right on time, I was ringing her doorbell. As I waited for her to open the door, I expected to meet a nice, understanding person who, after a few minutes of talking, would give me a donation and then I'd be on my way. I was in for a surprise.

When the door opened, I was greeted by an angry "lady" yelling at me and waving one of our flyers in my face. She basically screamed at me, asking how I expected her to believe what was on the flyer! She continued with her rant and told me cystinosis was not even a real illness because she had never heard of it. "It's all made up," she said, "So you can get people to donate and you can pocket the money!!!"

I was floored. Nearly speechless, I assured her it was a real illness because my son had it and I even directed her to a couple websites to prove it. She told me the websites were also created by me to make my lie even more believable. I ended this rant by saying, "Ma'am, if you don't feel comfortable donating, then please don't." I then left her step and drove home.

I have not seen or spoken to this "lady" since and now that my anger has far gone, I do feel I owe her a huge debt of gratitude. For it was her that gave me a true look as to just how much work needed to be done. There is still a great need for raising awareness and educating the public about this illness. If not for her, I'm not sure I would have continued my quest to change the future of this illness. I was convinced to never do another fundraiser again, due to the amount of work it took to do our first. Now we have just completed our third and most successful one yet. If not for her, I would likely never have known that cystinosis was so unheard of. If not for her, I would not be where I am today. If not for her, I may have given up.

So to the lady in the big brick house.....thank you! Thank you for doing what you have no idea you did!!

Where I Want to Be
By Amanda Leigh

"The greatest pleasure in life is doing what people say you cannot do."
Walter Bagehot

This was the first quote when I opened up the journal that I had gotten from a close friend of mine. A smile instantly broke out over my face. It was so fitting that this quote was the first one in that journal because it described me so well. I feel like I've been doing this my whole life. So many doctors didn't think that I would live past sixteen but here I am at twenty-six. Not only that, I have a high school degree, a Bachelor of Arts in English and Communications, I was the Assistant Managing Editor of my college literary magazine, I'm learning graphic design and I am an author. What's my point here? There have been many obstacles in my life but right now I am where I want to be. Is it 100% perfect? Well, I guess that would depend on your definition of the word "perfect." Nobody's life is perfect (at least no one I know) but it's important to focus on the good things in life. The things that we are thankful for.

I've wanted to be an author since I was eight years old and here I am, doing just that. Now, am I a J. K. Rowling or James Patterson? No. But that's okay because I am doing what I love. Even when it's hard to do it's still what I love and I consider myself lucky to be doing it. I've been making up stories for as long as I can remember. When I was two years old I would tell my mom the stories and she would write them down. I'd draw the pictures. My first "book" was about Sailor Moon and Tuxedo Mask. Now, you're probably wondering, why am I talking about telling stories and writing in an anthology that is supposed to be about cystinosis? Well, some of the things that we can talk about in this anthology are ways to deal with things. How we dealt with them. I am a writer, author, whichever word you prefer, down to the core of my being. It is very much who I am so when I approached this project this is the angle that I ended up going to.

Stories have kept me going for a long time; stories of all types, really. Books (my favorite medium of storytelling), television shows, movies, music (yes, I count this), even art. There can easily be a story in a piece of art or a song. I love getting lost in a story. I love the characters from these stories. They are like friends to me. Just like my friends in real life. I can pick up a favorite book and oh look, there are Harry, Ron and Hermione. Or turn on the television and decide who I want to see today. Mulder and Scully? Dharma and Greg? Aaron Hotchner? Elijah Mikaelson? There are many more. It's like hanging out with old friends for me. And books give me a sense of security on top of the great story. I always have one with me. When I go to the doctor, I pretty much always have a physical book with me and if I need to I clutch it tight. I love books and I love storytelling. It seemed a pretty natural progression that I would write my own stories. And those characters are also like good friends to me. Writing stories (and poetry but especially fiction) is my favorite way to express myself. I also love art, photography, crafts, singing, cooking. These things are what I choose to do and they have helped me get through hard times in my life for well, all of my life.

It took me a long, long time to even begin to write this. I wouldn't say that I've spent my life avoiding the subject, exactly, because let's face it, it's rather unavoidable, isn't it? I didn't really avoid it, I just did my best to not focus all of my energy on it. For me, this turned out to be the best approach. If I focused all of my energy on it I don't know how I would ever get anything done. That is not to say that there aren't sometimes days that I have a hard time for one reason or another. And that's okay. I think the important part is to not dwell on it and pick yourself back up again. The next day, or in the next hour (I've had hours that aren't so good while others are great), dust yourself off and start again. It's okay to have off days (or weeks). The most important thing I've learned is not to dwell endlessly on them. They don't make you weak. It makes you strong to be able to go through them and get back up again.

I definitely haven't had it easy but I focus on the positive things in my life. Like I said above, I am an author. I actually did it. How amazing is that? Even with that, I can get caught up in everything that goes with it (there is a lot more than I thought) but when I really stop to think about it, it is absolutely amazing. My words and stories are out there in the world. And there are people who like them. People who are waiting for more. Waiting for me to publish something new. Really, how crazy is that? Add in that doctors didn't think I would make it to sixteen and that some of them didn't even think I would go to college? It's pretty darn incredible. And I'll be honest, incredibly satisfying that I have proven doctors wrong more than once. Hence the quote that started this story of mine. Don't get me wrong, I'm not saying to go directly against something your doctor says just to prove them wrong but they said I wouldn't live to sixteen and now I'm twenty six. Some said I wouldn't go to college. I got a BA in English. And I'm a published author. What I'm saying is, you can do more than you think you can do. It's okay to have some things that you can't do. It's okay to have limitations. But don't let those dictate your entire life. Your entire outlook on life. I've had to adapt multiple times in my life. I can't speak to everyone's situation. Cystinosis manifests differently and affects us differently. What I'm saying is to not let it take away your joy, your life. Remember, more likely than not, you can do more than you think you can.

The Day Amanda Was Diagnosed
By Christina Morey

It was February 16, 1992. After many tests over the course of 16 days in the hospital, the doctors called for a meeting in the conference room. I knew this couldn't be good.

Upon entering the conference room I saw six doctors sitting around one side of the large round table. We sat on the other side facing them. Starting on my left, there was a geneticist, a metabolic specialist, a gastroenterologist, an endocrinologist, an orthopedist, and a nephrologist. As the geneticist started talking I suddenly felt like I was floating above the room looking down on what was happening. She was explaining the genetics of how a baby inherits genes from her parents. The "me" that was floating above the room was saying, "Okay, I learned this in school. I get it. Please get to the point!" She was actually drawing a diagram! "Please, please, tell me what's going on!"

As she was explaining how my baby girl inherited a recessive gene from each of us, and that this was why she had infantile nephropathic cystinosis, I could feel the air escaping my lungs and I literally couldn't breathe. She went on to explain how the chances of being born with this awful disease are 1 in 200,000 births. Each of the doctors took a turn explaining how the disease would affect my baby. She will definitely need a kidney transplant by the age of 10. She will most likely not see her 16th birthday. It was more than I could take.

At some point the nephrologist, who was all the way to the right, kind of chuckled and said, "You had a better chance of winning the lottery." I couldn't believe what I'd heard. Again, as if watching from above, I was in disbelief as the "me" that was sitting at the table suddenly jumped up out of the chair and across the table at him. I had to be held back. How could a doctor be so insensitive? Why would he say such a thing? Did he really think this was a good time for making light of the situation? I was just told that my baby would be lucky to see her 16th birthday.

This day seems like it was yesterday, but at the same time it seems like a lifetime ago.

On May 18, 2017 my baby girl turned 26 years old. As I think about what a miracle this is, I am brought back to that day in 1992. "You had a better chance of winning the lottery," ... CORRECTION ... I did win the lottery, the day God gave me Amanda Leigh.

A Grandmother's Story
By Xênia Mota

My name is Xênia Mota and I live in Northeast Brazil, in the city of Fortaleza. I have a grandson who has cystinosis. His name is Yago, he is eleven years old.

He was diagnosed when he was 18-months-old, we spent a year trying to discover what Yago had. It was very difficult for us in the beginning, then we went to São Paulo, Instituto da Criança, to an appointment with the specialist, Dr. Maria Helena Vaisbich, and she confirmed cystinosis. Unfortunately, here in Brazil, many doctors do not know about cystinosis. It is us who try to clarify on the disease.

Yago needs to take electrolyte supplements all day, like the others patients, and also cysteamine. Many children do not receive adequate treatment to have a good quality of life. Sometimes it's a financial matter or ignorance of the families or lack of government support that makes it difficult to access both treatment and medicines.

Across the country, there are not enough doctors who are experts in cystinosis. The biggest concentration of treatment is in São Paulo. In some cities in Brazil, the doctors who are faced with cystinosis, seek to study to treat the patient, or send them to São Paulo, but it is not always so. At the time we are fighting with the federal government to get cysteamine and eye drops, through the justice. The high cost of the drug is the biggest impediment to our country that does not value health! Concerning Procysbi, we don't have access for all patients, because the cost is much higher than Cystagon.

What can I say about Yago? He is a very happy little boy, despite living with the disease. His routine is normal, even with all the medicines he takes. He practices swimming, he learns English, he goes to school and he plays with his friends! His favorite game is to play football and he loves to surf.

Yago is very aware of his history and he knows that one day he will need a kidney transplant and that will change his life for the better.

It was for Yago and almost 130 patients, that we have created here in Brazil the Support Group for Cystinosis. We have a very large country and the communication was very hard between us. Now we can have close contact to exchange ideas and experiences. Together we can be stronger to fight the impediments that appear on our walk, for example, have the right to receive Cystagon!

Lastly, I want to say that Yago has a very large living force and many dreams to be realized. We learned a lot with him and I told him that he is my hero. May God permit a long life to him and all the patients who live with cystinosis!

Doctor's Visits
By Rebekah Palmer

Please press a button for a ticket,
the sing-song automated voice replied
to the pressure of my mother's fingertips.
We parked the van at the Children's Hospital
went inside to take some tests
before enrollment for Kindergarten.
The ticket the machine spit out was presented
to the guardian of the physicians realm.
She stamped the words "University of Minnesota Medical
Center Fairview"
on that ticket.
discount parking rates
Every time we saw the doctor
we were saluted by the words
please press a button for a ticket.
Curled up in the back seat of the car,
I would rub sleep from my eyes after the alarm of
please press a button for a ticket.
They should have stamped "UMMCF" on my backside
given me a discount on the days of my life
recalling the numbers
of missing calendar days because of the anthem

please press a button for a ticket
echoing in my ear.

Your Daughter Has
By Rebekah Palmer

Your daughter has cystinosis.
What's cystinosis?
It's not just a rare label; it's a rare disease.
Only two thousand people worldwide,
only five hundred living in America.
One. In five hundred. Living.
What does cystinosis do?
Her body no longer transports
proteins cell to cell;
crystals form on her
kidneys, eyes, muscles
pancreas, brain, liver
her body is slowly shutting down.
What will happen to my daughter?
Oral medication
Six hours. All day. Every day.
Her kidneys will need
to be replaced someday
for quality of life
to enjoy school and relationships
as others her age.
What should my daughter do?
Anything.
Cystinosis only has the power to hinder,
Interrupt, upset but
you and your daughter have the power
to persevere,
change,

keep swallowing medicine
as you live,
fight this disease.
One. One of two thousand.

Me and the Clock
By Rebekah Palmer

Ten am medicine 11 am noon pills with lunch
1 pm 2 pm 3 pm 4 more medicine 5 pm stomach
aches 6 pm supper more pills 7 pm 8 pm 9 pm
10 last dose of medicine 11 pm sleep all the
way 'til morning when it starts all over again
don't forget to take your eye drops on the top
of each waking hour.

Piano Player
By Rebekah Palmer

The patterns of black and white keys
the high melodies, the low basses, and every note in
between
depressed and elated days of a medical patient
float through the screened window into our neighborhood.
The high, glorious moment when side effects
aren't making themselves known and
low, bitter hours of screaming silently
to myself as pain covers my mouth and
won't let me speak become this song:
the harmonious and guttural music
coming from the belly of the kidney transplant patient.

Do You Work?

By Rebekah Palmer

"Do you work?"
What kind of question is that?
The way they ask it
it should be rephrased
"Do you have a job from 8 to 4?"
because anything else I answer
will be responded to with displeasure
or the other question
"Well, what do you do?"
Does that really matter?
Will what I do tell you who I am?
Here's what I do:
I wake up in the morning
to take medication
that leaves my stomach rancid
until the next dose
that leaves me bound to the clock
to make sure everything is taken
within the right amount of time
to prevent overdose until
the final handful of pills
tells me it's time to sleep again
to take a needed break before
morning comes and I must repeat
this little regimen again.
"Do you work?"
"Yes. Yes I do."
"Where?"
"From home. It takes effort
to keep me standing here answering
questions that make my head hurt
and wonder if who I am is a waste of space."

Out There
By Rebekah Palmer

Wanting to live outside my 5 senses,
my diseased body's walls,
looking at able-bodied men and women
seemingly living a life free from restraint
not realizing that I have created my own way
of experiencing life's joys and hardships.

Not realizing that my perception of
breathing and feeling have heightened my 5 senses
to a full life, fuller than theirs.

I see the beauty in living each second of
life to the greatest extent
I hear the joy in every rustle of leaves, in every bird's
twitter,
in every rush of wind as tires drive by my house on the
highway
I taste the goodness in each spoonful of ice cream,
in each cheese covered chip dipped in homemade salsa
I feel love in every warm embrace
I smell sweetness in soap suds of hot baths and
desire in Spring's lilacs and cherry tree blossoms.

For in their lack of bodily imprisonment
they know not that they are limitless to be,
to express, to do
they are mortal, they are dying
in total ignorance
so they cannot experience the ecstasy of knowing
how fast these moments fleet
and they cannot savor
the enjoyment of their

present lives…
they are imprisoned by life
while I am free.

Terminal Illness
By Rebekah Palmer

Love is like a curing medicine
and I am taking the pill.

Experienced are the following
side effects:

a beautiful soul has joined with mine
gentle words stroke my ears,

I am a separate body
with an orbiting moon

basking in warmth
and triboluminescence.

Rare Disease Rhapsody
By Rebekah Palmer

Cystinosis interrupts life
wrapped in a cloak of invisibility

lurking in every corner of your mind
it steals as if it were a thief

joy and peace become commodities
with the sleight of a wizard's cunning hand

the dark arts deviously mastered
Cystinosis makes a normal life disappear

in its wake a nightmare midnight deep
as sleep is disturbed to pour medicines like

potions to heal the body of this rot.
If ease would come visit me

and time would let me breathe
a big gulp of freedom

I would weep a sigh of relief so loud
the stars in the sky would sigh in reply.

Life with Amanda Panda

By: Suzanne Quartucio
Aunt of Amanda Leigh

It is said that "only an aunt can give hugs like a mother, keep secrets like a sister, and share love like a friend." (Spanish Proverb) This is the relationship that I've had with my niece, Amanda, since she was a baby.

Amanda is 26 years old now. 26! Such a miracle! Especially since the doctors said she would not see the age of 16 when she was diagnosed with nephropathic cystinosis at the age of 9 months.

I have been with Amanda and her mother (my sister) at many blood draws, doctors' appointments and hospital stays. I have also gone on some of the trips to see Dr. Gahl and his team at NIH in Maryland. On those trips I was the driver, the bag carrier, the photographer, the coffee buyer and the all-around-helper. But, most of all I was Amanda's moral support.

When Amanda started to make trips to NIH as a baby,
The Children's Inn had huge panda bears in the lobby.
This was so fitting for Amanda Panda! I have taken
pictures of Amanda with those pandas over the years.

I am so grateful for The Children's Inn and the wonderful
people that work there. Staying there has always made
the long trips to NIH "bearable" for my Amanda Panda.

Our Winning Team
Mauricio + Marcela = Antonia

By: Mauricio Quijano
Father of Antonia Quijano Vargas, 4 years old.

Michael Jordan said, "Talent wins games, but teamwork and intelligence win championships." In our case, we play a lifetime championship against a rival called cystinosis. A rival who weakens us physically by not letting us sleep more than four hours and also emotionally when we receive test results with levels that we do not expect.

But in all tournaments teams become stronger; new hires are made and training day to day allows us to move with more agility on the court. Once we know the game rules like strict compliance with medication schedules, supplements, eye drops, and medical visits with the nephrologist, ophthalmologist, nutritionist, gastroenterologist and others, we start to score goals against our rival.

"Levels of potassium and creatinine are normal." Point for us.

The top players on this team are our children, who with their courage in blood tests, their patience when they receive nutrition and medicine by their G-tube at night, their discipline with eye drops and their smile against different situations, constantly encourage the rest of the team and are the inspiration to keep scoring points.

In the case of those who play this tournament in Latin America like us, we face many additional challenges, such as controlling treatment without the possibility of periodic white blood cell (WBC) cystine tests, some doctors on our teams did not know about cystinosis until our children visited their offices, a culture that lacks support of causes through donations and the barriers that sometimes appear to authorize life-saving medications are some of our issues that make us stronger but unfortunately threaten our tranquility and the stability of our children.

However the team motivation does not fail, we strengthened the defense with the best weapon: love. Constantly we illuminate the path of the other players with a light, the light of hope represented by those members who work to improve treatments and, of course, find a cure, which will win this championship against cystinosis.

Antonia
Our story with Antonia is not very different from other children with cystinosis. With my wife Marcela we've been through a process where the doubts took over our lives and the constant search for what was wrong with her health became our only goal.

Fortunately we do not travel alone, a whole army of angels have joined us and their support, knowledge and positivity have made everything easier.

One of our biggest challenge as parents has been to provide security to our daughter while we make her days like any other child's. Her stomach button is a part of her life (just as someone uses glasses to see better), medicines are part of her routine and even she is the one who tells us that it is cystagon time when the alarms sound.

Our greatest reward is to get up every morning and see her beautiful smile which makes us feel that all this effort is worthwhile.

Colombia
In our country there are about 20 registered cases, seven of which are part of the "Valiant Group" that we create to stay in touch, share information, medications, stories, but above all, to give support and fight for better conditions for our children. Right now, our main challenges are bringing the eye drops to Colombia and implementing the WBC cystine test.

Gradually we have been moving forward on some of these issues. The support of members from the cystinosis community in other countries is very valuable to us and the foundations in the United States who have listened to us and connected us with laboratories and physicians who are always willing to help give us hope.

This championship we play against cystinosis has brought us many lessons as a family, it strengthens our faith daily, but most importantly, makes us admire our beloved children, who are the real stars of our team.

What Cystinosis Means to Me

by Kathleen Roberts, age 15

If I were to be brutally honest I would say that I didn't really start thinking about cystinosis, and what it meant to me, until around the time I was finishing grade 8. Before that it was just sort of there, in the back of my head. It still is in a way. Of course I knew all the basic medical facts, or as much as a thirteen and half year old can understand at that point (which is a lot more than one would think). And I would say my knowledge was fairly good. But the thing is, I never really truly thought about it much.

For example, I remember sitting on my window bench in my room when I was around 7 or 8 years old. A family friend and her parents were over and she was about the same age as me. At one point she started saying her parents had told her something about me that seemed very big to her. I had no idea what she was talking about. When she realized this she didn't want to tell me in case I didn't know. I persisted in getting the information out of her. It ended up being that I would need a kidney transplant in the future. My answer? "Yea that's true. So what? Let's keep playing Barbies." It was honestly no big deal to me although it obviously was for her. My medical condition and future medical needs wasn't something I obsessed over. It just was, and still is, my normal.

But since then I have started thinking about cystinosis more and, with time, I've realized that I have actually become grateful for it. Don't get me wrong, I would way rather be a healthy teenage girl, but I have found that cystinosis has given me perspective on life.

What would I tell someone to expect from cystinosis? Well, some days are going to be horrible. That's the plain truth. Those are the kind of days where this disease beats the shit out of you and all the worst feelings that come along with it tangle up in a knot, pulsing and begging for your attention. You will experience tiredness, anger, hatred, a 'why me' attitude and a whole plethora of conflicting emotions. But the thing is these days aren't as often as you would think. In fact they're few and far between. The less you let cystinosis take over your life, the less often you will have those days. You have to fit cystinosis into your life and not let it eat up everything in its path. Acknowledge the challenge and adjust. It's okay to feel frustrated or have a few bad days. In fact it's probably better for your sanity. But you have to get up and move on and let yourself live.

I can also tell you that this challenge, or however you would like to think of cystinosis, can bring gifts in disguise. It gives you empathy and an understanding that everyone has their obstacles in life, even if you can't see them. Everything is in relation to something else. A problem that may seem small to you, may seem enormous to someone else. It goes the other way too. Sure cystinosis is a hard illness but there are thousands of other people with harder lives. And, in my opinion, all problems count and should be acknowledged. Cystinosis will give you strength and endurance, if not of the body then of the mind. It teaches you to be grateful for what you have and gives you opportunities to meet amazing people you would otherwise have never met. It also will bring friends and family closer when it really counts.

I guess what I'm trying to say is, like a lot of things in life, cystinosis has many, many different sides to it. Some of it you can be told and some of it you have to discover for yourself. I still don't know what cystinosis really means to me or how I really feel about it. I could say it differs from day to day, situation to situation. And I think that is probably the most accurate description. I will likely be figuring it out for the rest of my life, as its meaning to me is always evolving. The one thing I can say for certain is you have to hold on to hope no matter how fragile it seems to become. And when cystinosis puts you in a hard position try not to say, "Why me," but instead say, "Try me".

My Brother Florian

By Isabelle Rodriguez

Translated by Fiona W.

My name is Isabelle Rodriguez, I'm 20 years old and I have a younger brother named Florian, 16, who has Cystinosis.

His illness was discovered when he was 2 years old; until that age there were never any issues but when he started losing weight and refusing to eat, my parents became worried and wanted to know what was wrong. The results came in the summer of 2001, Florian had cystinosis.

When I was younger, I was amazed by the number of pills he had to take, it was a lot for one person, and with time, other problems came. Autism (the doctors never knew where that came from), skin problems, and the most 'serious' of all - osteoporosis. When he was around 6 or 7, he started to limp. The doctor didn't listen to us and, as nothing was done, he ended up in a wheelchair. He had two operations to try to help him to walk again but, even though he managed to take a few steps, he was very scared.

The illness didn't stop changing. He became more and more fragile and we didn't know why. His autism stopped him from communicating with us, to tell us if he felt pain somewhere, and I think this caused some more problems.

In July 2015, he had several attacks of epilepsy and, once again, we don't know where that came from, and his state of health became worse with time. He passed away on the 4th October 2015 due to an infection. He fought for 16 years against an illness and it was a virus that finally took him.

Today I'm still in a sort of depression because I'm having a lot of trouble dealing with his death. My brother was my whole life and I would have given anything if it meant that nothing ever happened to him and that he stayed in good health.

I hope this story will show people how brave he was, because he really was. In my eyes, he was the bravest boy in the whole world.

My Story
By Serena Scott

Hi, my name is Serena; I'm 34 years young although some days I feel older than my grandparents. I was born a "normal baby" until I turned 18 months old. Yep you know the story, after 2 months of being in hospital I was diagnosed with this annoying disease called "cystinosis!"

I tell people that my life is like a rollercoaster. One minute my life is up and great and the next it goes down. When I was 8 years old my beautiful mum donated me a kidney, she said it was like putting a brand new battery in my body, I was all go! My mum is very special to me, she is always there for me and I love her so much.

During my teens I suffered from feelings of loneliness and depression as I didn't know anything or anyone with cystinosis. I started getting super bad migraines which put a lot of stress on me as I didn't know why I was getting them. Doctors said it was inherited from my family. Super, so I now had 2 inherited diseases.

I took a lot of medications, which I hate doing, but in my mind's background, I hear my mum saying "you must take your medications baby girl or you will die," so obediently I take them!

My life went from good to bad over night as I was rushed to hospital with a migraine and wasn't seen for 7 hours in emergency. That experience I will always remember! That episode I lost my voice for 6 weeks due to vomiting. I was deeply upset as a speech therapist told me she was unsure I would ever get my voice back as she thought I had torn my vocal cords. Sure enough after a very long 6 weeks I got my voice back but it wasn't the same. That was 10 years ago, and my speech is getting worse. Doctors say it's part of cystinosis, but who knows? Now my muscles are also deteriorating so I find it hard to open jars, chop foods to eat, I get quite weak and lethargic and so very tired most days.

I've had some highlights in my life too. In 2002 I attended my very first cystinosis conference. I met many other people just like me and I felt happy! I was no longer alone in this big world.

Since 2002 my mum and I have set up the Australian and New Zealand support group where we fundraise and help other cystinosis families in need. I have also attended four other international cystinosis conferences in Ireland, Italy, Paris and Manchester! I'm currently fundraising to get to my sixth conference in Spain this year. I have also set up an adults Facebook group just for adults to talk.

I have achieved a lot in my life, although I would have liked to achieve much more, but I take each day as it comes. I try to stay as positive as I can because life can get you down fast when looking on all the negatives.
I love exercise and going to the gym, and shopping is my favourite hobby. I inherited a good gene off my mum and that is I love creating things, cooking, crafts, gardening, they are a few of my specialties. Whatever life throws at me I will continue to fight.

My Story
By Bryan Stout

I have always believed that God puts people in our lives for a reason. I have met a handful of extraordinary people who have the same disease I do, cystinosis. I think that we are all part of a small community (less than 550 in the US) to help encourage one another, rather it be sharing our experiences, asking questions, or simply being an example for the younger ones affected.

I was diagnosed at 18 months, and remember a pretty normal childhood other than some frequent hospital visits, a lot of terrible tasting medication, throwing up on many occasions, and drinking tons of water. Cystinosis is not a fun disease by any means, but I don't want this whole story to be about that. It affects my life, but in no way does it define me.

I am the oldest of 4 so of course my family is very important to me. Growing up I was lucky, my brother and 2 sisters helped me with my crazy medication routine! Even with being smaller than most of the other kids my age, and the stinky side effects from the medicines, I rarely dealt with bullying, simply because my siblings always had my back. My parents never treated me differently, and I was raised just like the rest of the crew.

Around age 9 I had to go on dialysis due to my low kidney function. I honestly don't remember it being that bad. My mom learned to do the whole process at home overnight. One time in particular I remember we taped a plastic bag to my stomach just so I could get into the ocean! Nothing was going to stop me from joining in and having fun! After almost 3 years of dialysis, I got the call for a new kidney! Duke was about 3 hours away and we made it there in 2! We actually beat the kidney there! Once I received a transplant, I felt like a new kid, almost instantaneously, and gained a pretty sweet scar. I used to tell kids at the pool that I had got bitten by a shark, gotta have a sense of humor! I always wanted to wrestle and play football, but my doctors wouldn't let me because of my kidney; probably a good call because I have now had this kidney for 24 years! But anyway, I decided to go with softball and basketball. Yes even being this short, I played basketball!

Probably the hardest thing I have ever faced was when I was around 16 years old; I would wake up gasping for air. But, during the day, when I was awake, I could breathe perfectly normal. The doctors could not figure it out. So, after numerous ER visits, I eventually had to have an emergency tracheostomy; it was extremely scary! For some reason, my vocal chords would collapse during any relaxed state, causing me to have difficulty breathing. Doctors never decided whether it was cystinosis related or due to the many times I'd been put to sleep as a child, possibly rupturing my vocal chords in the process and making them weak. I had the trach tube for over 6 years and yes, it sucked!

The most important lessons I've learned when going through anything difficult is; one, have faith. Two, always have a sense of humor, and three, aways remember somebody out there has it worse than you do! My parents have always kept me laughing at something during the tough times. I was told I would have to keep the breathing tube most likely for the rest of my life, but with our faith (lesson one) we prayed about it and got a second opinion. The very first day I was told by the new doctor he could get rid of the trach tube! We were blown away! I had two options to choose from and went with the second, which was 6 vocal cord surgeries to take a little out at a time; in turn making me a bit hoarse but no stupid tube in my neck! Afterwards I felt like a new man! For days I stayed in the pool and lake, trying to make up for the years of fun I'd missed!

Now in my early 20's I felt pretty good, healthwise. I decided to attend my very first cystinosis conference. I met a handful of people around my age who were pretty similar to me, I became particularly close to a few who seemed to live life like I did. Over the years I always kept in touch with them. Sadly one of the very first people I met passed away and that really affected me. She is no longer suffering and in a much better place, but she was a sweetheart and a very close friend of mine. Her passing kind of drew me closer to the community, I guess you could say. I have attended more conferences since and become closer to some individuals. I like helping out in any way possible, including having been on a few adult panels to help spread positivity and hope. As I said before there are truly some incredible individuals with this extremely rare disease, and they too give me hope! Some of them I consider my closest friends. Because of my disease I have actually been privileged to travel around the US and attend some very special events, I otherwise would never have been a part of. So I am very thankful for that.

My parents are definitely two of the strongest people I know. They've been together for over 30 years now. My mom is where I get my strength from, having beat stage 3 breast cancer and never slowing down. She has taught me to be feisty and never give up. She raised 4 kids with very little help. I watched my dad struggle financially for years; he worked 2 and 3 jobs to give all 4 of us the absolute best growing up. Anytime I would go through a rough patch, he was always there to lighten up the moment and make me laugh. He is definitely where I get my sense of humor from. If they didn't like a doctor's answer, they found another one, never giving up. So thankful for them both!

In college I studied horticulture, which I really enjoyed. Even won an award for being in the top 3 of my class! I've also volunteered at a local hospital for a few years, which also was a neat experience. I would love to travel to Ireland one day and hope to make it back to LAMBEAU! But by far my biggest accomplishment in life is being an uncle! I have 5 nephews and two nieces now! They are my world. I see a few of them almost every day. They definitely keep me busy and entertained! It's pretty simple, I just want to have a positive impact on their lives and be a good example.

I'm 35 now and in pretty good health, although a battle with sepsis a few years ago has really affected my kidney. I may have to get a new one in a year or so. But I have faith and a big family full of possible donors! Now if the new kidney will only last as long as this first one! I

have plenty of hope and determination for the future!
GOD Bless!

*"It's not the years in your life that count,
it's the life in your years."*
Abraham Lincoln

Acknowledgements

We would like to thank:

Katie & Jeff Larimore for agreeing to work with us on this project and for all of their hard work over at the CRN.

Jose Morales & Christy Greeley: for working with us on the logistics and technical aspects of this project. We're glad you are just as excited.

Dr. Paul Goodyer: for writing the foreword to this book. We know how busy you must be and appreciate that you took the time.

Christina Morey: for formatting the final version of this book. It looks beautiful.

Claire Johnston: for your help with marketing this book.

And thank you to everyone who contributed and shared the news about our exciting project!!

Epilogue

When first given the diagnosis that you or someone you love has a rare disease one can feel incredibly shocked and isolated. The doctors' visits and treatments can be a heavy burden to bear and the world may suddenly seem bleak. We hope that this collection has shed some light and shown the many facets of life with a rare disease. The cystinosis community may be small in number but we are a family, full of support and compassion. To have so many people willing to share their stories truly touched us and we hope this collection does justice to their bravery. In addition to raising awareness this collection will also help change the prognosis of cystinosis with all proceeds going directly to the Cystinosis Research Network.

We hope that even if you have not been affected by cystinosis you got something out of this collection. Life is filled with ups and downs, light and dark. Everyone and everything is beautiful in some way. And often broken in some way. But don't overlook the beauty in the broken. Maybe this book can shed some hope on a dark time for you. Maybe you'll refer to it again and again. Find stories of courage, life and hope within these pages. Don't ever turn away from the light in the darkness.

The Cystinosis Research Network was established in April 2001. It is an all-volunteer, non-profit organization dedicated to supporting and advocating research, providing family assistance and educating the public and medical communities about cystinosis. With a vision to accelerate the discovery of a cure, improve treatments and enhance the quality of life for those with cystinosis.

Their commitment to the cystinosis community includes tireless efforts to provide family assistance through facilitating support groups, hosting family conferences, town hall meetings, and more. A beacon of hope and support within the cystinosis community, the Cystinosis Research Network has been an incredible resource and something to hold on to for so many of us.

For more information and to support the Cystinosis Research Network go to www.cystinosis.org

About Amanda Leigh:

Amanda Leigh has had a love of words since before she could write them herself. Once she learned to read and write herself she just couldn't stop. She reads any genre as long as the book sounds interesting. Which may explain why she can't and never will be able to stick to one genre in her writing. From Contemporary Romance to Women's Fiction to Paranormal Romance to Poetry and more to come. When she's not writing or reading she enjoys getting swept away in a great TV show, going to the theater, listening to music, cooking and many different forms of art. She has a cat she adores and also loves Psychology, tea, coffee, chocolate and Elvis Presley. Not necessarily in that order. Feel free to get in touch with her.

Visit Amanda Leigh online at:
https://authoramandaleigh.com/

About Amanda Buck:

Amanda Buck is a mother to two beautiful children and began writing after her daughter was diagnosed with cystinosis. She started the blog Elsinosis: Living with Cystinosis to chronicle their story, advocate for her daughter and help other families in similar situations look for their silver linings. Her writing has appeared on the online community blogs such as the Good Mother Project, The Mighty and Coffee + Crumbs and she was a cast member of Vancouver's inaugural Listen To Your Mother Show. You can also follow her family's story on her blog and social media.

Visit Amanda Buck online at: https://elsinosis.com/

40338907R00073

Made in the USA
Middletown, DE
25 March 2019